IN THE NICK OF TIME

*W*hat could be better than an old-fashioned homemade Christmas? But with today's hectic pace, many of us don't have a lot of time for extensive preparations. This year, you can create the celebration of your dreams no matter how much (or how little!) time you have to spare. In the Nick of Time *is* filled with quick and easy ideas to guide you through every aspect of the holidays, from decorating the house to creating thoughtful gifts and delicious holiday dishes. There's even a full menu for a Christmas dinner that leaves you extra time to enjoy the day! We've used the latest time-saving techniques (such as hemming a table topper with fusible web tape instead of needle and thread) to help you finish holiday trimmings and handmade gifts quick as a wink. And using purchased mixes and convenience foods lets you whip up Yuletide treats in half the time. Join us for a wonderful family celebration!

Anne Childs

LEISURE ARTS, INC.
Little Rock, Arkansas

EDITORIAL STAFF

Editor-in-Chief: Anne Van Wagner Childs
Executive Director: Sandra Graham Case
Executive Editor: Susan Frantz Wiles
Publications Director: Carla Bentley
Creative Art Director: Gloria Bearden
Production Art Director: Melinda Stout

DESIGN
Design Director: Patricia Wallenfang Sowers
Designers: Donna Waldrip Pittard, Diana Heien Suttle, Linda Diehl Tiano, and Rebecca Sunwall Werle

FOODS
Foods Editor: Celia Fahr Harkey, R.D.
Assistant Foods Editor: Jane Kenner Prather
Test Kitchen Assistant: Nora Faye Spencer Clift

TECHNICAL
Managing Editor: Kathy Rose Bradley
Senior Editor: Kimberly J. Smith
Technical Writers: Chanda English Adams, Emily Jane Barefoot, Leslie Schick Gorrell, Candice Treat Murphy, Linda Luder, Cathy Hardy, Lois Phillips, and Katherine Satterfield Robert

EDITORIAL
Associate Editor: Linda L. Trimble
Senior Editorial Writer: Terri Leming Davidson
Editorial Writer: Tammi Williamson Bradley
Copy Editor: Laura Lee Weland

ART
Book/Magazine Art Director: Diane M. Ghegan
Senior Production Artist: Michael A. Spigner
Art Production Assistant: M. Katherine Yancey
Photography Stylists: Karen Smart Hall, Christina Tiano, and Charlisa Erwin Parker

ADVERTISING AND DIRECT MAIL
Senior Editor: Tena Kelley Vaughn
Copywriters: Steven M. Cooper, Marla Shivers, and Jonathon Walker
Designer: Rhonda H. Hestir
Art Director: Jeff Curtis
Production Artists: Linda Lovette Smart and Angie Griffin
Typesetters: Cindy Lumpkin, Stephanie Lindersmith, and Larry Flaxman

BUSINESS STAFF

Publisher: Steve Patterson
Controller: Tom Siebenmorgen
Retail Sales Director: Richard Tignor
Retail Marketing Director: Pam Stebbins
Retail Customer Services Director: Margaret Sweetin
Marketing Manager: Russ Barnett

Executive Director of Marketing and Circulation: Guy A. Crossley
Fulfillment Manager: Byron L. Taylor
Print Production Manager: Laura Lockhart
Print Production Coordinator: Nancy Reddick Lister

Library of Congress Catalog Number 94-75390
International Standard Book Number 0-942237-38-2

Table of Contents

TRIMS IN A TWINKLING......................6

CHEERY COUNTRY KITCHEN 8
  Country Kitchen Tree....................14
  Redbird Ornaments.......................14
  Country Swag...........................14
  Redbird Tree Skirt......................15
  Cedar Topiaries.........................15
  Sock Stockings..........................15

A GOLDEN CELEBRATION 16
  Swirl Ornaments.........................18
  Tussie-Mussie Ornaments..................18
  Marbleized Ornaments.....................18
  Lacy Gift Wrap..........................18
  Angel Wall Hanging......................18

EASY ELEGANCE 20
  Elegant Table Runner....................22
  Pouf Table Skirt with Tasseled Topper.........22
  Mantel Scarf............................23

HOMESPUN CHARM......................24
  Rag-Trimmed Tree........................26
  Rag Ball Ornaments......................26
  Rag Wreath Ornaments....................26
  Homespun Tree Ornaments.................26
  Crocheted Fabric Tree Skirt...............28

VISIONS OF SUGARPLUMS 30
  Gingerbread House Centerpiece.............32
  Gingerbread House Ornaments..............32
  Gingerbread Girl and Boy Ornaments...........33
  Party Favors 33

WELCOMING WREATHS 34
  Partridge in a Pear Wreath................36
  Teddy Bear Wreath.......................36
  Season's Greetings Wreath................36
  Double-Loop and Multi-Loop Bows...........36

RUSTIC SANTA......................37
  Fence Post Santa 37

A TOUCH OF VICTORIANA 38
  Decoupaged Ornament 42
  Decorated Candles 42
  Crazy Quilt Tree Skirt 42
  Christmas Cards and Envelopes...............42

GIFTS IN A JIFFY...............................44

HEARTWARMING MUFFLER SET 46
  Gingerbread Warmers
POINSETTIA WRAP-UP...........................48
  Padded Pot Cover
CHEERY CHRISTMAS TOWELS 49
  Country Kitchen Towels

PILLOW DRESSING 50
  Wrap Pillow Cover
  Ribbon-Tied Pillow Cover
  Appliquéd Pillow Cover
GLITZY SNEAKERS...............................52
  Red Sequined Sneakers
  Snowflake Sneakers
  Green Plaid Sneakers

Table of Contents

PRETTY POINSETTIA APRON 53
  Pretty Poinsettia Apron
CHRISTMASTIDE CANDLE TINS 54
  Wintry Candle Tins
CAROLER'S SWEATSHIRT 56
  Christmas Candles Sweatshirt
ABC BUTTON COVERS 57
  Shiny Apple Button Covers
FESTIVE FOOTWEAR 58
  Festive Socks
YULETIDE FRAMES 60
  Padded Christmas Frame
  Christmas Box Frame
ELEGANT AFGHAN 62
  Double-Strand Diamond Afghan

CHRISTMAS PAPER ART 65
  Christmas Paper Art
SNOWY "IN-VEST-MENT" 66
  Easy Appliquéd Vest
CANDLELIGHT PLACE MATS 67
  Candlelight Place Mats
MERRY MEMORY ALBUMS 68
  Covered Photo Albums
CANDYLAND FUNWEAR 70
  Choo-Choo Sweatshirt
  Cookies and Candy Cardigan
COZY COASTERS 72
  Christmas Tree Coasters
NORTH WOODS THROW 73
  Rustic Christmas Throw

TREATS IN A WINK 74

FOR YOUR "DEERS" 76
  Nutty Maple Fudge
  Reindeer Basket
CHRISTMAS PIE 77
  Chocolate-Covered Cherry Pie
  "Happy Christmas" Pie Pan
CORDIAL SNOWMAN 78
  Raspberry Cream Liqueur
  Snowman Bottle Bag
"HOLLY-DAY" BREAKFAST 80
  Bacon-Mushroom Casserole
  Holly Table Runner
POPCORN GIFT TIN 82
  Nutty Butterscotch Popcorn
  Decorated Popcorn Tin
SAUCY POINSETTIAS 83
  Jezebel Sauce
  Napkin Rings and Jar Cover

ROLL OUT THE ELEGANCE 84
  Dried Fruit-Nut Rolls
  Fruit Roll Wrap
  Decoupaged Plate
GRANOLA GOODIE BOXES 86
  Chocolate Granola Candies
  Yo-Yo Shaker Boxes
"BEARY" JAM 88
  Berry Christmas Jam
  "Beary" Bag
PEPPERMINT TOTES 90
  Chocolate-Dipped Peppermint Sticks
  Christmas Mini Totes
CRUNCHY MUNCHIES 92
  Curried Snack Sticks
  Snow Scene Gift Tin

Table of Contents

GINGERBREAD DELIGHT 93
  Gingerbread Bars
  Gingerbread Box
"GLOW WINE" 94
  Glühwein
  Bargello Mug
TINS OF TREATS....................................96
  Cranberry-Orange Jelly
  Christmas Candy Lollipops
  Button-Trimmed Gift Tins
CHRISTMAS SNACK SACKS 98
  Rocky Road Candy
  Fruitcake Cookies
  Reindeer Gift Bag
  Santa Gift Bag

DELIGHTFUL QUICK DISHES 100
  Cranberry Freezer Daiquiris 102
  Sweet-and-Sour Pork Chops 102
  Southwest Olive Bread.............................102
  Stuffed Gouda Cheese 102
  Cheesy Crab Toasts..................................103
  Zesty Ripe Olive Dip 103
  Cheese Danish Pastries...............................104

Chocolate Cinnamon Rolls 104
Nutty Fudge Pie 105
Spiced Coffee Mix......................................105
Brownie Nut Bread.....................................106
Creamy Cinnamon Spread 106
Holiday Ice Cream......................................107
Champagne Punch 107

FAST AND FESTIVE FARE 108
  Turkey and Dressing Ring 110
  Green Beans au Gratin 110
  Herbed Christmas Rolls..............................110
  Fruited Sweet Potato Casserole 111
  Cranberry-Orange Gelatin Salad 111
  Fudge-Topped Pumpkin Pie 113
  Apricot-Nut Fruitcake................................113
  Raspberry Cider 113

PATTERNS 114
GENERAL INSTRUCTIONS 123
KITCHEN TIPS 124
RECIPE INDEX 126
CREDITS..127

TRIMS IN A TWINKLING

Decorating for Christmas is a time-honored tradition, but it doesn't have to take a lot of time! This year, turn to our oh-so-easy ideas for decorations reflecting the most beloved of all Christmas images, from angels and Santas to redbirds and gingerbread houses. You'll use shortcuts and simple techniques to create beautiful ornaments, wall hangings, and other accessories to deck your home in holiday style — and no one will guess how fast each one was for you to make!

CHEERY COUNTRY KITCHEN

The natural beauty of a country celebration abounds in this charming collection. Designed to brighten a kitchen or dining area, these simple decorations recall the holidays of years past, when everyday items were often transformed into festive accents. We've mirrored those cozy celebrations with our fast-to-finish designs, created by combining basic items from the cupboard with simple supplies from the craft shop. May the warmth of this home-style Christmas touch your heart with good cheer!

Providing color and charm, padded fabric cardinals are easy to craft with a little machine stitching and a bit of glue. Heart-shaped aluminum gelatin molds are spruced up by gluing on fabric heart cutouts and buttons. Winding around the tree, sprigs of red-berried greenery add splashes of vibrant color. Purchased punched-metal ornaments and raffia bows are natural finishing touches.

10

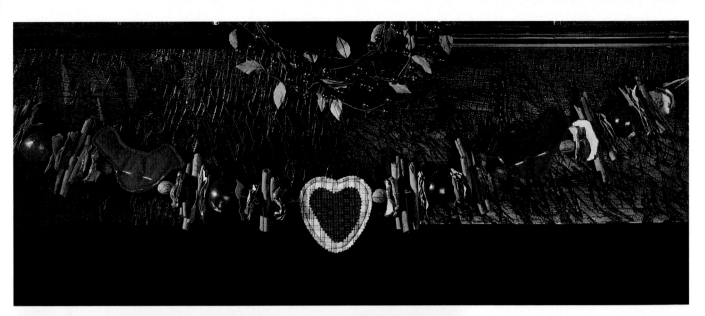

The goodness of a country kitchen is reflected in this fragrant swag for a mantel or window. No one will guess how easy it was to assemble with whole nutmegs, cinnamon sticks, bay leaves, preserved apple slices, handcrafted redbirds, and other simple items.

Our cheery theme is continued with a heartwarming no-sew tree skirt. The circle of plaid fabric is cut along the edge with pinking shears and fused to felt for a super-quick finish. And the "stitches" on the stenciled designs are actually made with a felt-tip pen!

Resembling miniature Christmas trees, our cedar topiaries make it fun — and easy — to spread holiday spirit all through the house. These quick craft projects are created by gluing preserved cedar to cone-shaped topiary forms. For a touch of whimsy, we trimmed one of them with a bright redbird ornament. (Opposite) The festive cuffs of our homey stockings are really tubes of plaid fabric tucked into the tops of heavy socks. Clipped to the cuffs, personalized clothespin hearts will help Santa know whose goodies to put in each one.

COUNTRY KITCHEN TREE

(Shown on page 8)

This charming tree adds a bit of country to Christmas. Leafy sprays of bright red berries, wired to the branches to resemble garland, bring a touch of the outdoors to this 3½-foot-tall tree. Redbird Ornaments (this page) perched throughout the tree are easy and quick to make with a little sewing and gluing. Tiny heart-shaped gelatin molds become ornaments when fabric hearts cut with pinking shears and buttons are hot glued inside; for hangers, hot glue a knotted loop of jute twine to the top of each mold. The raffia bows and purchased punched-tin house ornaments give a rustic look to the tree, and the easy stenciled Redbird Tree Skirt (page 15) wrapped around the base of the tree completes this cozy scene.

REDBIRD ORNAMENTS (Shown on page 10)

For each ornament, you will need two 6" squares of red fabric, one 6" square of polyester bonded batting, fabric scrap for wing, 6" of ¹⁄₁₆"w satin ribbon (for hanger; optional), black thread, pinking shears, fabric glue, tracing paper, and a removable fabric marking pen.

1. Use small bird and wing patterns and follow **Tracing Patterns**, page 123.
2. For bird, use fabric marking pen to draw around bird pattern on right side of 1 red fabric square (backing).

3. Place batting on wrong side of remaining fabric square; place backing right side up on batting and pin layers together.
4. Use black thread to machine stitch along drawn lines. Leaving an approx. ¼" seam allowance, use pinking shears to cut out bird.
5. For wing, use pattern to cut wing from scrap fabric. Glue wing to bird.
6. If hanger is desired, fold ribbon length in half to form a loop; glue ends of loop to back of bird.

WING

SMALL
BIRD

LARGE
BIRD

COUNTRY SWAG (Shown on page 11)

For an approx. 50" long swag, you will need 62" of jute twine, 8 whole nutmegs, 16 dried apple slices, 24 cinnamon sticks, bay leaves, 4 artificial pomegranates, four 6½" red fabric squares for redbirds, two 6½" fabric squares for heart, a 5" fabric square for heart center, three 6½" squares of polyester bonded batting, paper-backed fusible web, ⅛" hole punch, hand-held craft drill, pinking shears, tracing paper, black thread, large needle, and craft glue.

1. Use large bird and large and small heart patterns and follow **Tracing Patterns**, page 123. Use large bird and large heart patterns and follow Steps 2 - 4 of Redbird Ornaments instructions to make 2 birds and 1 heart. For heart center, draw around small heart pattern on paper side of web. Follow manufacturer's instructions to fuse web to wrong side of heart center fabric. Use pinking shears to cut out heart along drawn lines.

2. Use hole punch to punch 4 holes in large heart (**Fig. 1**) and 4 holes in each bird (**Fig. 2**).

Fig. 1

1¼"

Fig. 2

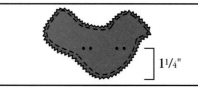

1¼"

3. Carefully drill a hole through center of each nutmeg, cinnamon stick, and pomegranate.
4. Thread needle with jute twine; thread twine through holes in heart, centering

heart on twine. Glue twine to back of heart to secure. Remove paper backing from heart center. Center and fuse heart center to front of large heart, covering twine on front of heart.
5. Thread 1 nutmeg, 2 apple slices, 3 cinnamon sticks, several bay leaves, 1 pomegranate, several more bay leaves, 3 more cinnamon sticks, 2 more apple slices, and another nutmeg onto each end of twine and position close to heart.
6. With each redbird facing center of swag, thread redbirds onto twine next to nutmegs. Repeat Step 5 to complete swag, positioning added items close to birds. Knot each end of twine after last nutmeg.
7. For each hanging loop, fold end of twine 6" to 1 side; knot twine approx. 2½" from fold.

SMALL HEART

LARGE HEART

14

REDBIRD TREE SKIRT (Shown on page 11)

You will need a 40" square of fabric, a 42" square of felt, five 5/8" dia. buttons, paper-backed fusible web, removable fabric marking pen, pinking shears, string, hot glue gun, glue sticks, a thumbtack or pin, acetate for stencil, craft knife, red and green acrylic paint, stencil brushes, paper towels, removable tape (optional), black permanent felt-tip pen with fine point, and cutting mat or thick layer of newspapers.

1. Follow manufacturer's instructions to fuse web to wrong side of fabric square; remove paper backing. Matching right sides, fold fabric square in half from top to bottom and again from left to right.

2. To mark outer cutting line, tie 1 end of string to fabric marking pen. Insert thumbtack through string 18" from pen. Insert thumbtack in fabric as shown in **Fig. 1** and mark 1/4 of a circle.

Fig. 1

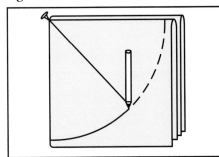

3. To mark inner cutting line, repeat Step 2, inserting thumbtack through string 11/2" from pen.

4. Cutting through all layers of fabric, use pinking shears to cut out fabric along marked lines.

5. Follow Step 1 of **Stenciling**, page 123, to make bird, branch, and heart stencil.

6. To stencil design, position heart of stencil straight up-and-down with bottom of heart 1/2" from outer edge of fabric. Using red paint for bird and heart and green paint for branch and leaves, follow Step 2 of

Stenciling, page 123, to stencil 1/2 of design. Clean stencil and turn stencil over. With heart of stencil positioned over painted heart on fabric, stencil remaining half of design.

7. Leaving approx. 21/4" between designs, repeat Step 6 to stencil design 5 more times along outer edge of skirt.

8. Use black pen to outline designs and to draw dashed lines close to edges of hearts, birds, and leaves to resemble stitches.

9. Using a pressing cloth, fuse skirt to felt. Use pinking shears to trim felt to 1/2" from outer edge of skirt and even with inner edge of skirt. For opening in back of skirt, fold skirt in half along centers of 2 stenciled hearts; cut along 1 fold from outer edge to inner opening.

10. Hot glue 1 button to center of each whole heart.

CEDAR TOPIARIES
(Shown on page 12)

For each topiary, you will need desired size plastic foam cone (ours measure 9", 12", and 16" high), 8" of a 1/2" dia. wooden dowel, green acrylic spray paint, clay flowerpot (we used 31/4", 41/4", and 5" high pots), floral foam to fit in pot, Spanish moss, preserved cedar, raffia, hot glue gun, glue sticks, and 1 Redbird Ornament without hanger (page 14; optional).

1. Spray paint cone green; allow to dry.

2. Glue floral foam into pot to within 1/2" of rim. Cover foam with Spanish moss.

3. For trunk, insert dowel approx. 3" into cone and approx. 3" into foam in pot.

4. Working from bottom to top of cone, glue preserved cedar to cone.

5. Tie raffia into a bow around pot.

6. If desired, glue Redbird Ornament to topiary.

SOCK STOCKINGS
(Shown on page 13)

For each stocking, you will need a men's size 9-11 wool sock, a 12" x 16" fabric piece for cuff, thread to match fabric, a 21/8"w wooden heart cutout, acrylic paint and paintbrush to paint heart (optional), Design Master® glossy wood tone spray (available at craft stores and florist shops), spring-type clothespin, black permanent felt-tip pen with fine point, safety pins, hot glue gun, and glue sticks.

1. For cuff, match right sides and long edges and fold fabric piece in half. Using a 1/2" seam allowance, sew long edges together to form a tube. Press seam allowance open. Turn tube right side out. Fold bottom raw edge of tube to inside to meet top raw edge; press.

2. Place raw edges of cuff 4" into sock; use safety pins to secure. Fold cuff down over sock.

3. For hanger, lightly spray clothespin with wood tone spray; allow to dry. Paint heart or lightly spray heart with wood tone spray; allow to dry. Use pen to write name on heart and to draw dashed lines along edge of heart to resemble stitches. Glue heart to clothespin. Clip clothespin to cuff.

A GOLDEN CELEBRATION

When the Magi presented their gifts to the Newborn King, they introduced gold as a precious element in the Yuletide celebration. You'll find it easy to continue that tradition with our opulent collection of golden accents. By simply adding touches of paint or brilliant trims to purchased pieces, you can quickly enrich your holiday decorating and adorn your home with splendor!

Our elegant tree radiates richness with a variety of adornments. Glass ornaments are spray-painted and drizzled with metallic paints or marbleized and topped with silk and dried flowers for two distinctive finishes. Add a little romance with our miniature Victorian tussie-mussies — they're really spray-painted ice-cream cones filled with flowers! Using paper doilies as stencils makes lacy gift wrap a breeze to paint. Top your packages with gold wired ribbons for a dazzling flourish. (Opposite) Herald the holiday with this graceful wall hanging. Cut from gold lamé fabric, the angels are fused to a damask background and then accented with golden trims, ribbons, and a floral spray.

SWIRL ORNAMENTS

(Shown on page 17)

For each ornament, you will need a glass ornament, desired color spray paint (we used gold or bronze), 2 coordinating dimensional paints in squeeze bottles with fine tips (we used gold and dark brown), and gold trim for hanger.

1. Spray paint ornament; allow to dry.
2. (**Note:** Practice painting technique on a paper plate.) Holding tip of dimensional paint bottle approx. 1" from ornament and applying constant pressure to bottle, rotate ornament slowly under line of paint to create swirls as desired. Repeat with a second color of paint. Hang ornament to dry.
3. For hanger, thread a length of gold trim through ornament hanger and knot ends together.
4. To store, wrap each ornament individually in tissue paper.

TUSSIE-MUSSIE ORNAMENTS

(Shown on page 17)

For each ornament, you will need a small cone-shaped ice-cream cone (ours measure 4 1/4" long); metallic gold spray paint; 7/8" long gold fringe; 13" of 1/16" dia. gold twisted cord; dried flowers; silk flowers, leaves, and berries; hot glue gun; and glue sticks.

1. Spray paint cone gold; allow to dry.
2. Glue fringe along top edge of cone, trimming to fit.
3. Arrange leaves, flowers, and berries in cone; glue to secure.
4. For hanger, knot and fray each end of cord; glue 1 knot to each side of cone approx. 1 1/2" below top edge.

MARBLEIZED ORNAMENTS

(Shown on page 17)

For each ornament, you will need a frosted glass ornament; acrylic paints (we used bronze, light gold, gold, and dark brown); denatured alcohol (available at drugstores or paint supply shops); small pieces of cellulose sponge; aluminum pie pan; artificial flowers, leaves, and berries; 1/8" dia. gold twisted cord; hot glue gun; and glue sticks.

1. Dampen 1 sponge piece; use sponge piece to stamp entire ornament with 1 color of paint. Without allowing paint to dry between colors, repeat with remaining paint colors.
2. Before paint dries, hold ornament over pie pan and pour a small amount of alcohol over ornament. Lightly blow on ornament to spread and mix paint colors until desired effect is achieved. Hang ornament to dry.
3. Tie a length of cord into a bow; knot and fray ends. Glue bow to ornament. Glue flowers, leaves, and berries to ornament over bow.
4. For hanger, thread a length of cord through ornament hanger and knot ends together.

LACY GIFT WRAP

(Shown on page 17)

You will need white paper, assorted paper doilies (we used 4" dia. doilies), 1/2"w gummed stars, metallic gold spray paint, removable tape, and stick glue.

1. Place paper on a protected surface; tape in place. Arrange doilies on paper as desired; use stick glue to lightly hold doilies in place. Lightly adhere stars to paper.
2. Spray paint paper gold; allow to dry.
3. Carefully remove doilies and stars from paper.

ANGEL WALL HANGING

(Shown on page 16)

You will need a 24" square and a 27" square of beige damask fabric for wall hanging; two 10" squares of dark gold lamé fabric and four 6" squares of light gold lamé fabric for angels and wings; 2 1/8 yds each of 2 1/2"w and 1 1/2"w wired ribbon and 1 1/4 yds of 1/8" dia. gold twisted cord for bow; assorted gold trims for edges and circle on wall hanging; two 5" lengths of 7/8" long gold fringe for bottoms of robes; 7/8 yd of 1/16" dia. gold twisted cord and two 2 1/2" long gold tassels for hanger; 25" of 3/8" dia. wooden dowel; dried flowers; silk flowers, leaves, and berries; metallic gold dimensional paint in squeeze bottle; paper-backed fusible web; 3/4"w paper-backed fusible web tape; fabric marking pencil; tracing paper; drawing compass; handsaw; fabric glue; hot glue gun; and glue sticks.

1. Follow manufacturer's instructions to fuse web to wrong side of 24" fabric square. Remove paper backing. Matching wrong sides, center 24" fabric square on 27" fabric square; fuse in place.
2. Follow manufacturer's instructions to fuse web tape along each side edge on wrong side of large fabric square. Do not remove paper backing. Lightly press side edges of large fabric square to wrong side along edges of small fabric square. Unfold edges and remove paper backing. Refold edges and fuse in place. Repeat with top and bottom edges.
3. Trace angel and wing patterns, page 19, onto tracing paper and cut out.
4. For angels, fuse web to wrong side of each 10" dark gold lamé fabric square. Use pattern to cut 1 angel from each square, cutting 1 in reverse.
5. For wings, fuse web to wrong sides of two 6" light gold lamé fabric squares; remove paper backing. Matching wrong sides, fuse squares to remaining 6" squares.

Use wing pattern to cut 1 wing from each fused square, cutting 1 in reverse.

6. For circle pattern, use compass to draw a 12" dia. circle on tracing paper; cut out. Use fabric marking pencil to draw around circle pattern at center front of wall hanging.

7. (**Note:** Refer to photo for remaining steps.) Arrange angels over sides of drawn circle; fuse in place.

8. Use dimensional paint to outline angels and to paint details on angels; repeat for right side of each wing. Allow to dry.

9. For each angel, refer to patterns and match ● and ◆ on wing to ● and ◆ on angel; use 2 dots of hot glue to secure wing.

10. (**Note:** Use fabric glue for gluing unless otherwise indicated. Allow to dry after each glue step.) Cut lengths of trim to cover remainder of drawn circle; glue lengths in place. Repeat to glue another circle of trim 1" outside first circle.

11. Glue lengths of fringe along bottom edge of each angel's robe.

12. Glue trim along edges of wall hanging. Glue a second line of trim approx. 1" inside trim along edges, angling trim at corners.

13. Tie ribbon lengths together into an approx. 7"w bow; trim ends. Hot glue bow to top of circle over trims. Tie 1/8" dia. cord into an approx. 6"w bow; knot and fray

ends. Hot glue cord bow to ribbon bow. Arrange streamers of bows on wall hanging; hot glue in place.

14. Arrange leaves, flowers, and berries beneath bows and at bottom of circle; hot glue in place.

15. For hanger, hot glue 1 tassel to each end of 1/16" dia. cord. Use saw to make a 1/2" notch in each end of dowel. Insert dowel through sleeve formed by seam at top of wall hanging. With tassels hanging just below dowel, hot glue cord into notches in dowel.

ANGEL

WING

EASY ELEGANCE

Drape your home with elegant fabric accents this season — all without sewing a stitch! Designed to enhance rooms throughout your home, each beautiful piece is made in no time using fabric glue and easy-to-use fusible web tape. By mixing and matching festive textiles in bold prints or stately plaids, you'll find it easy to bring out the splendor of your holiday decor.

Cover an inexpensive decorator table with a majestically poufed table skirt. Created by simply tucking the edges under and arranging the folds, the skirt is topped with a square of tartan plaid tied at the corners with opulent cord and tassels.

A length of plaid fabric in gilded Christmas colors becomes a dramatic mantel scarf when trimmed with luminous gold braid and bows. To form the elegant points, simply cut vertical slits in the fabric, fold each section to a point, and fuse in place. What could be easier!

Dress up your holiday feast with this beautiful table runner crafted in a splendid print. Fast to make, it's hemmed with fusible web tape and then accented with glued-on trim and wired-ribbon bows.

ELEGANT TABLE RUNNER
(Shown on page 21)

You will need fabric, 5/8"w gold scalloped trim, 1 1/2 yds of 1 1/2"w gold mesh wired ribbon, 1/2"w paper-backed fusible web tape, fabric glue, fabric marking pencil, and 2 safety pins.

1. Add 1" to desired finished length of runner. Cut fabric 16"w by the determined measurement.

2. Referring to **Fig. 1**, use fabric marking pencil to draw a point on wrong side of fabric at each end of runner. Cut fabric along drawn lines.

Fig. 1

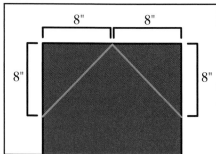

3. To hem edges of runner, follow manufacturer's instructions to fuse web tape along edges on wrong side of fabric. Do not remove paper backing. Lightly press short edges, then long edges, to wrong side along inner edge of tape. Unfold edges and remove paper backing. Refold edges and fuse in place. Secure corners with glue.
4. Beginning and ending at 1 end of runner, glue trim along edges on wrong side of runner with scalloped edge of trim extending beyond edges of runner.
5. For bows, cut ribbon in half. Tie each length into a bow; trim ends. Using safety pins on wrong side of runner, pin 1 bow to each end of runner.

POUF TABLE SKIRT WITH TASSELED TOPPER (Shown on page 20)

For table skirt for round table, you will need fabric, 1"w paper-backed fusible web tape, and fabric glue.

For table topper, you will need fabric, 1"w paper-backed fusible web tape, four 4 1/4" long gold tassels, 1 1/4 yds of 1/4" dia. gold twisted cord, 4 safety pins, and fabric glue.

TABLE SKIRT

1. Refer to **Diagram** to measure table and drop length; add 40". Cut a square of fabric the determined measurement (if necessary, use web tape to piece fabric).
2. To hem skirt, follow manufacturer's instructions to fuse web tape along edges on wrong side of fabric square. Do not remove paper backing. Lightly press edges to wrong side along inner edge of tape. Unfold edges and remove paper backing. Refold edges and fuse in place. Secure corners with glue.
3. Center skirt on table. Tuck edges of fabric under at floor and arrange folds for "pouf" effect.

TABLE TOPPER

1. Measuring to desired drop length of table topper, refer to **Diagram** to measure table and drop length; add 2". Cut a square of fabric the determined measurement (if necessary, use web tape to piece fabric).
2. To hem topper, follow manufacturer's instructions to fuse web tape along edges on wrong side of fabric square. Do not remove paper backing. Lightly press edges to wrong side along inner edge of tape. Unfold edges and remove paper backing. Refold edges and fuse in place. Secure corners with glue.
3. (**Note:** To prevent ends of cord from fraying after cutting, apply fabric glue to 1/4" of cord around area to be cut, allow to dry, and then cut.) Cut cord into four 11 1/4" lengths. For each corner of topper, measure 9" from corner and gather fabric; use a safety pin on wrong side of fabric to secure gathers. Wrap 1 length of cord several times around gathered area; secure with glue. Wrap hanging loop of tassel around wrapped cord and glue top of hanging loop to top of tassel.

DIAGRAM

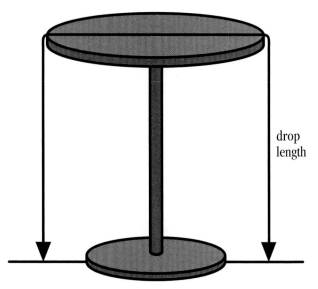

drop length

MANTEL SCARF (Shown on page 21)

You will need medium weight fabric, 1/2"w paper-backed fusible web tape, 1/8"w flat gold trim, 1 1/4"w gold mesh ribbon, fabric marking pencil, and fabric glue.

1. Measure length of mantel and add 1"; measure width of mantel and add 9 1/4". Cut fabric the determined measurements.
2. To hem short edges (sides), follow manufacturer's instructions to fuse web tape along each short edge on wrong side of fabric. Do not remove paper backing. Lightly press each edge to wrong side along inner edge of tape. Unfold edges and remove paper backing. Refold edges and fuse in place. Repeat to hem 1 long edge of fabric (back edge of scarf).
3. To determine width of points, match side edges and fold fabric in half; fold in half again. Repeat until desired point width is reached (our points are 8 1/2" wide; we recommend making points between 5" and 10" wide). Record width of folded fabric and unfold.
4. (**Note:** Refer to **Diagram A** for Step 4.) For points, use fabric marking pencil and a ruler to draw a horizontal line 6 1/2" from long raw edge on wrong side of fabric. Beginning at 1 side edge, use point width determined in Step 3 to draw vertical lines from first drawn line to raw edge of fabric.
5. (**Note:** Refer to **Diagram B** for Step 5.) Fuse web tape along raw edge of fabric, along each side edge from horizontal line to first piece of web tape, and along each side of each vertical line from horizontal line to first piece of web tape. Remove paper backing.
6. Cut along each vertical line up to horizontal line. Mark bottom center of each cut section.

7. Referring to **Figs. 1** and **2**, fold side edges of each cut section to wrong side from horizontal line to marked center point; finger press folds and trim excess fabric. Fuse in place.

Fig. 1

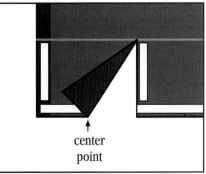

center point

Fig. 2

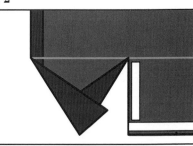

8. Glue trim 1/8" from bottom edge on right side of scarf. Allow to dry.
9. For bows, subtract 1 from number of points on scarf. Cut the determined number of 22" lengths of ribbon. Tie each length into a bow; trim ends. Glue bows to scarf between points; allow to dry.

DIAGRAM A

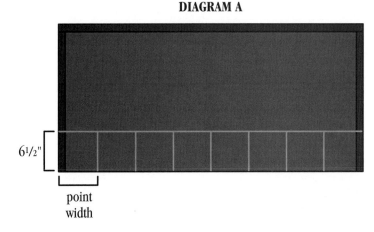

6 1/2"

point width

DIAGRAM B

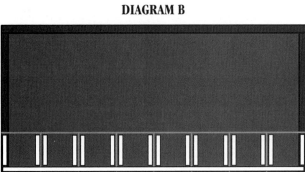

23

HOMESPUN CHARM

Enjoy the simple beauty of a homespun holiday with these charming decorating ideas. All of our country trims are fun to make using easy craft techniques and coordinating fabric strips. You can even crochet a festive tree skirt in no time using a colorful blend of Christmas reds and greens. You won't believe how easy it is to create this home-style celebration!

Old-fashioned rag ball ornaments are quick to craft by gluing fabric strips onto foam balls and topping them with homespun bows. Our frayed-fabric tree motif, stitched onto a square of muslin, makes a special gift accent or cute tree ornament. Using fabric strips and easy single and double crochet stitches makes the homey tree skirt fast to work. (Opposite) If you can tie a knot, you can make dozens of wreath ornaments like this one in no time! Just tie fabric strips around a jar lid band and then glue on a bow and button for a fast, festive finish.

25

RAG-TRIMMED TREE

(Shown on page 25)

With its easy fabric decorations, this tree provides the backdrop for a simple homespun Christmas. First, red wooden bead garland and pretty bows tied from 1¼"w fabric strips are tucked among the branches. Folksy Rag Ball Ornaments (this page) are easily crafted by covering plastic foam balls with red and green fabric strips. Super-easy Rag Wreath Ornaments (this page) are made by covering canning jar lid bands with more fabric strips. Miniature baskets filled with baby's breath and embellished with glued-on buttons add a natural touch to the tree. Resembling patchwork blocks, Homespun Tree Ornaments (this page) can trim a package or hang from a branch. Providing the final handcrafted touch, the Crocheted Fabric Tree Skirt (page 28) brings to mind an old-fashioned crocheted rug adorning the floor of a country home.

RAG BALL ORNAMENTS

(Shown on page 25)

For each ornament, you will need a 3" dia. plastic foam ball, coordinating fabrics to cover ball and for bow, fine nylon thread, sewing needle, hot glue gun, and glue sticks.

1. To cover ball, cut approx. fifteen ½" x 10" strips from fabrics. With strip right side out and using a small drop of glue, glue 1 end of 1 fabric strip to foam ball (top of ornament). Wrap strip around ball and glue remaining end over first end. Overlapping long edges of strips, repeat to cover ball completely.
2. For bow, cut three ½" x 14" strips from fabrics. Tie strips together into a bow. Glue bow to top of ornament, covering ends of strips.
3. For hanger, thread needle with 8" of nylon thread and take a stitch through center of bow. Knot ends of thread together.

RAG WREATH ORNAMENTS

(Shown on page 24)

For each ornament, you will need a 3" dia. (wide-mouth) canning jar lid band, coordinating fabrics for wreath and bow, a ½" dia. button, hot glue gun, and glue sticks.

1. For wreath, cut approx. thirty-six ¾" x 7" strips from fabric. Loosely tie strips around jar lid band, covering entire band.
2. For bow, cut a ¾" x 20" strip from fabric. Tie strip into a bow; trim ends. Glue bow to wreath. Glue button to bow.

HOMESPUN TREE ORNAMENTS

(Shown on page 25)

For each ornament, you will need a 6½" square of red print fabric for backing, a 7" square of muslin for front, four 6" squares of green print fabrics for tree, a 1" x 2" fabric piece for trunk, paper-backed fusible web, ½"w paper-backed fusible web tape, ¾ yd of ⅛"w green satin ribbon, red embroidery floss, vegetable brush, fabric glue, and tracing paper.

1. For tree, trace patterns, page 27, onto tracing paper; cut out. Pin 6" green print fabric squares together. Cutting through all layers, use patterns to cut tree top and tree bottom from fabric squares.
2. For each section of tree, trim third fabric layer approx. ⅛" smaller all around than bottom fabric layer. Using third layer as a guide, repeat to trim second layer. Using second layer as a guide, repeat to trim top layer. Layer pieces of each tree section from largest to smallest as shown in **Fig. 1**. Cut slits in bottom of each layered section as shown in **Fig. 2**.

Fig. 1

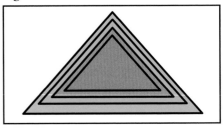

Fig. 2

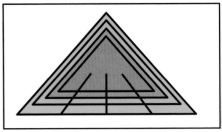

3. Follow manufacturer's instructions to fuse web to wrong side of muslin square and tree trunk fabric piece; do not remove paper backing. Cut a 5¹/₂" square from muslin and a ¹/₂" x 1¹/₄" piece from tree trunk fabric.

4. (**Note:** Refer to photo for remaining steps.) Position muslin square with 1 corner at top. Overlapping sections approx. ³/₄", arrange top and bottom sections of tree on muslin square with top of top section of tree approx. 1¹/₂" from top corner of muslin; pin in place.

5. Using 6 strands of floss, use **French Knots**, page 123, to attach tree sections to muslin square. Use vegetable brush to gently fray edges of tree sections.

6. For tree trunk, remove paper backing from fabric piece and fuse piece to muslin with 1 end of trunk ¹/₄" under bottom section of tree.

7. Remove paper backing from muslin. Being careful not to press tree, fuse muslin square to center of wrong side of backing fabric square.

8. Follow manufacturer's instructions to fuse web tape along each edge of wrong side of backing fabric square; do not remove paper backing. Lightly press edges to wrong side (toward muslin) along inner edge of tape. Unfold edges and remove paper backing. Refold edges and fuse in place. Use glue to secure corners.

9. For trim on ornament, cut four 5¹/₂" lengths of ribbon. Glue ribbon lengths over raw edges of backing fabric.

10. For hanger, fold remaining ribbon in half to form a loop; glue ends of loop to back of ornament.

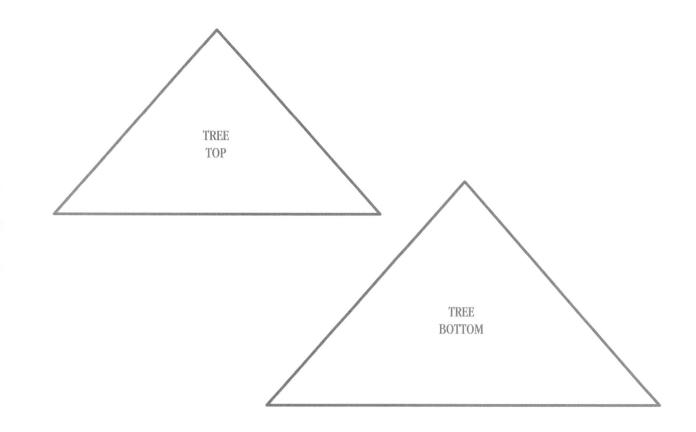

TREE
TOP

TREE
BOTTOM

CROCHETED FABRIC TREE SKIRT (Shown on page 25)

GENERAL INSTRUCTIONS
ABBREVIATIONS

approx.	approximately
ch(s)	chain(s)
dc	double crochet(s)
mm	millimeters
sc	single crochet(s)
sp(s)	space(s)
st(s)	stitch(es)
w	wide
YO	yarn over

★ — work instructions following ★ as many **more** times as indicated in addition to the first time.

( ) — work enclosed instructions **as many** times as specified by the number immediately following **or** contains explanatory remarks.

GAUGE

When crocheting with fabric strips, gauge doesn't matter that much; the finished piece can be a little larger or smaller without changing the overall effect. However, tension must be maintained throughout to make piece lie flat.

PREPARING FABRIC STRIPS

Fabrics selected should be high quality evenweave 100% cotton **or** cotton blend, such as those sold for piecing quilts. Yardages given are based on 44/45"w fabrics.

If fabric is not pre-shrunk, it should be gently machine washed and dried before tearing. Straighten fabric by pulling it across the bias. It may be necessary to lightly press fabric.

Tear off selvages. Tear fabric in 1¹/₂"w strips. To avoid joining fabric strips often, we recommend that fabric strips measure 2 yards long or longer.

JOINING FABRIC STRIPS

The following is a technique for joining fabric strips without sewing strips together; this eliminates knots or ends to weave in later.

1. To join a new strip of fabric to working strip, cut a ¹/₂" slit approx. ¹/₂" from end of each fabric strip (**Fig. 1**).

Fig. 1

2. With **right** sides up, place end of new strip over end of working strip and match slits (**Fig. 2**).

Fig. 2

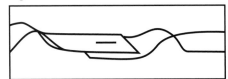

3. Pull free end of new strip through both slits from bottom to top (**Fig. 3**).

Fig. 3

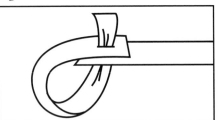

4. Pull new strip firmly to form a small knot (**Fig. 4**). Right sides of both strips should be facing up. Continue working with new strip.

Fig. 4

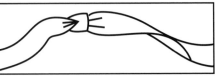

FREE LOOPS OF A CHAIN

When instructed to work in free loops of a chain, work in loop indicated by arrow (**Fig. 5**).

Fig. 5

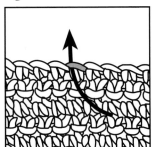

BACK LOOP ONLY

Work only in loop(s) indicated by arrow (**Fig. 6**).

Fig. 6

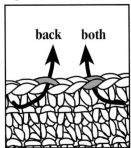

SINGLE CROCHET (abbreviated sc)

Insert hook in st or sp indicated, YO and pull up a loop, YO and draw through both loops on hook (**Fig. 7**).

Fig. 7

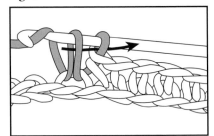

DOUBLE CROCHET (abbreviated dc)

YO, insert hook in st indicated, YO and pull up a loop, YO and draw through 2 loops on hook (**Fig. 8**), YO and draw through remaining 2 loops on hook (**Fig. 9**).

Fig. 8

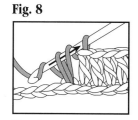

Fig. 9

MATERIALS

100% cotton or cotton blend fabrics, approximately:

Green Print - 3 pounds Mill End Strips
    OR 12 yards

Red Print - 2½ pounds Mill End Strips
    OR 10 yards

Ecru - 1 pound Mill End Strips
    OR 4 yards

Solid Red - 1 pound Mill End Strips
    OR 4 yards

Crochet hook, size P (10.00 mm)
Yarn needle

INSTRUCTIONS

Note: Read General Instructions, page 28, before beginning project.

PANEL A (Make 4)

Row 1: With Green Print ch 2, sc in second ch from hook.

Row 2 (Right side): Ch 1, turn; 2 sc in sc.

Note: Loop a short strip of fabric around any stitch to mark last row as **right** side.

Row 3: Ch 1, turn; sc in first sc, 2 sc in last sc: 3 sc.

Rows 4-22: Ch 1, turn; sc in each sc across to last sc, 2 sc in last sc: 22 sc. Finish off.

EDGING

With **right** side facing and working in ends of rows, join Ecru with slip st at end of Row 22; ch 1, sc in same row and in next 20 rows; 3 sc in free loop of beginning ch (**Fig. 5, page 28**); sc in next 21 rows; finish off: 45 sc.

PANEL B (Make 3)

Work same as Panel A, working Rows 1-22 with Red Print and Edging with Solid Red.

ASSEMBLY

Note: Panels are joined in the following order: A-B-A-B-A-B-A.

Position two panels with **wrong** sides together. Using Ecru, sew through both pieces once to secure the beginning of the seam, leaving an ample end to weave in later. Working through inside loops of stitches along edges of both pieces, insert needle from **back** to **front** through first stitch and pull fabric through (**Fig. 10**), ★ insert needle from back to front through next stitch and pull fabric through; repeat from ★ across, leaving center sc of 3-sc group unworked.

Fig. 10

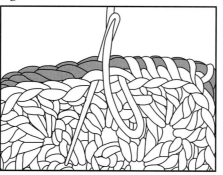

BORDER

Row 1: With **right** side facing and working in Back Loops Only of Row 22 (**Fig. 6, page 28**), join Red Print with slip st in first sc on first Panel; ch 1, sc in same st and in next 21 sc, ★ sc in end of next row and in next joining, sc in end of next row and in Back Loop Only of next 22 sc; repeat from ★ across; finish off: 172 sc.

Row 2: With **right** side facing and working in Back Loops Only, join Green Print with slip st in first sc on Row 1 of Border; ch 1, sc in same st and in next 8 sc, 2 dc in each of next 3 sc, ★ sc in next 22 sc, 2 dc in each of next 3 sc; repeat from ★ across to last 10 sc, sc in last 10 sc; finish off: 193 sts.

Row 3: With **right** side facing, join Ecru with slip st in last sc on Edging of first Panel; ch 1, sc in end of next row, ch 1, place marker around ch-1 just made for Row 4 joining; working in Back Loops Only across sts on Row 2 of Border, sc in first sc, ch 1, (skip next st, sc in next st, ch 1) across; working in ends of rows, skip next row, sc in next row, ch 1, slip st in first sc on Edging of last Panel; finish off.

Row 4: With **right** side facing, join Solid Red with slip st in marked ch-1 sp; ch 2, (sc in next ch-1 sp, ch 2) across to last 2 ch-1 sps, slip st in next ch-1 sp, leave last ch-1 sp unworked; finish off.

Tie: With Green Print, chain a 50" length; finish off.
Weave Tie through unworked sc at top of each Panel.

Bows: Tie a 1³⁄₈" x 20" strip of contrasting fabric to center of Row 20 on each Panel. Tie strips into bows; trim ends.

Visions Of Sugarplums

With these delightful designs, you can bring all the fun of traditional gingerbread to your holiday decorating — without all the baking or mess! We've made it easy to craft the whimsical "confections" using poster board, paper doilies, and dimensional paint. So charmingly simple, these accents will be fun to display year after year.

Nestled amid a forest of miniature trees, this gingerbread house is a charming centerpiece that could tempt even Hansel and Gretel! Its intricate look is easily made by gluing paper doily "icing," button "windows," and garland "shrubs" onto a purchased papier mâché house. Complete the scene with ribbon and miniature toy candy canes.

These "delicious" party favors couldn't be easier! Just use dimensional paints and miniature artificial candies to create adorable pins from wooden cutouts. Then attach them to bags of Christmas candies for sweet surprises.

Decking the tree with gingerbread treats will delight children of all ages! Simply paint details on poster board shapes to make these cute gingerbread boy and girl ornaments. Cardboard pieces, covered with bits of paper doilies, buttons, and miniature artificial candies, make charming gingerbread house ornaments. Finish the tree with a purchased "candy" garland for trims that look good enough to eat!

GINGERBREAD HOUSE CENTERPIECE (Shown on page 30)

You will need a 5"w x 11"l x 7¼"h papier mâché house; two 12" square white paper doilies; Design Master® glossy wood tone spray (available at craft stores and florist shops); white, iridescent white, red, and green dimensional paint in squeeze bottles; assorted buttons; miniature artificial candy canes; wired miniature greenery garland for shrubs; satin ribbon to thread through doily on roof; craft glue; hot glue gun; and glue sticks.

Note: Instructions are written for house centerpiece decorated on all sides.

1. Lightly spray house with wood tone spray; allow to dry.

2. To cover roof, measure from 1 edge of 1 doily and cut a 5¼" x 12" piece from doily. Measuring from opposite edge of doily, cut another 5¼" x 12" piece. Fold cut edge of each doily piece ¼" to wrong side. Paint red dots along remaining edges of doily pieces; allow to dry.

3. For each doily piece, thread a length of ribbon through cutouts in doily piece; trim ribbon ends even with folded edge of doily piece. Use craft glue to glue ends in place.

4. With folded edges of doily pieces at top of roof, use craft glue to glue 1 doily piece to each side of roof. Allow to dry.

5. For each bow, tie a 14" length of ribbon into a bow and hot glue to roof. Arrange streamers and hot glue in place. Hot glue 1 button and 1 candy cane over end of each streamer.

6. Cut desired shapes from remaining doily to resemble doors, windows, and trim. Use craft glue to glue doors, windows, and trim to house; allow to dry.

7. Hot glue buttons and candy canes to house as desired.

8. For shrubs, bend lengths of garland as desired and hot glue to house.

9. Use white, red, and green paint to paint dots on windows and trim and around doors. Apply iridescent white paint along tops of shrubs to resemble snow. Allow to dry.

GINGERBREAD HOUSE ORNAMENTS (Shown on page 31)

For each ornament, you will need lightweight brown cardboard; a white square paper doily; Design Master® glossy wood tone spray (available at craft stores and florist shops); white, iridescent white, red, and green dimensional paint in squeeze bottles; assorted buttons; 2 miniature artificial candy canes; two 2" lengths of wired miniature greenery garland; 10" of ¼"w ribbon for hanger; tracing paper; craft glue; hot glue gun; and glue sticks.

1. Lightly spray cardboard with wood tone spray; allow to dry.

2. Trace gingerbread house pattern onto tracing paper; cut out. Use pattern to cut house from cardboard.

3. Cut 2 approx. ³/₈" x 2⁷/₈" strips from edge of doily. Use craft glue to glue strips to top edges of roof, trimming strips to fit. Cut desired shapes from doily to resemble window and door. Use craft glue to glue window and door to house. Allow to dry.

4. Hot glue buttons and candy canes to house as desired.

5. For shrubs, bend each garland length as desired and hot glue to house.

6. Use white, red, and green paint to paint dots on house. Apply iridescent white paint along tops of shrubs to resemble snow. Allow to dry.

7. For hanger, fold ribbon length in half, forming a loop; hot glue ends of ribbon to back of ornament.

GINGERBREAD
HOUSE

GINGERBREAD GIRL AND BOY ORNAMENTS (Shown on page 31)

You will need white poster board; Design Master® glossy wood tone spray (available at craft stores and florist shops); white, red, green, and black dimensional paint in squeeze bottles; graphite transfer paper; and tracing paper.

1. Lightly spray poster board with wood tone spray; allow to dry.

2. Trace gingerbread girl and boy patterns onto tracing paper. Use transfer paper to transfer patterns onto poster board desired number of times.

3. (**Note:** Refer to photo for Step 3. Allow to dry after each paint color.) For each gingerbread girl, use white paint to paint outlines of ornament and dress and dots for hair. Use red paint to paint mouth and dots for cheeks, buttons, and details on dress. Use black paint to paint eyes. For each gingerbread boy, use white paint to paint outlines of ornament, bow tie, shirt, and pants and dots for hair. Use red paint to paint mouth and cheeks. Use green paint to paint buttons. Use black paint to paint eyes.

4. Cut out ornaments.

GINGERBREAD GIRL

PARTY FAVORS

(Shown on page 31)

For each favor, you will need a 2"h gingerbread man-shaped wooden cutout, Design Master® glossy wood tone spray (available at craft stores and florist shops), white dimensional paint in squeeze bottle, red permanent felt-tip pen with fine point, miniature artificial candy, pin back, hot glue gun, glue sticks, clear cellophane gift bag, red metallic and white curling ribbon, a 5" dia. white paper doily, and treats to put in bag.

1. For gingerbread man pin, lightly spray gingerbread man cutout with wood tone spray; allow to dry. Use white paint to outline cutout and to paint dots for eyes and buttons; allow to dry. Use red pen to draw mouth. Hot glue miniature candy to cutout. Hot glue pin back to back of cutout.

2. Place treats in bag. Knot 1 length each of red metallic and white ribbon around top of bag. Gather doily across center to form a bow shape; place gathered area over knot of ribbon and knot ribbon again around doily. Curl ribbon ends. Pin gingerbread man pin to ribbon.

GINGERBREAD BOY

WELCOMING WREATHS

Why settle for plain wreaths when you can have unforgettable ones in minutes? The wreaths shown here, ranging from traditional elegance to fanciful fun, are just a few examples of how you can create a holiday wreath that's as unique as your family and your home!

Used in ancient Greece and Rome to bestow glory and tribute on men of honor, wreaths of bay leaves are especially symbolic adornments for celebrating the birth of Christ. A store-bought bay wreath gives you a head start on this festive decoration. Pinecones, pomegranates, berries, and other naturals are added with hot glue, and holiday greetings are hand-written on painted wooden hearts.

Take those playful teddies out of hibernation and set them loose on this whimsical wreath! Dressed in doll clothes, your bears can frolic with easy-to-craft pom-pom snowballs and purchased miniature sleds and shovels. A candy-striped bow and a scattering of artificial snow complete the winsome scene.

(Opposite) On the first day of Christmas, charm your true love with this "partridge in a pear wreath." To make it, start with a vine wreath and use hot glue to create a nest of silk poinsettias, greenery, pears, acorns, and other trims. Top it off with a wired-ribbon bow for an elegant flourish.

PARTRIDGE IN A PEAR WREATH

(Shown on page 34)

Natural, yet elegant, this 20" dia. vine wreath will add warmth wherever it's hung. We gave the wreath sparkle by using Rub'n Buff® to add golden highlights to white silk poinsettias, silk leaves, and artificial pears. Sprigs of preserved evergreen and boxwood; stems of assorted artificial berries, acorns, and pecans; and the highlighted flowers, leaves, and pears are hot glued to the wreath, providing a perfect "nest" for a 5" high artificial partridge. To add a finishing touch of color, we made a double-loop bow from 3½"w wired ribbon and wired it to the top of the wreath (see Double-Loop Bow instructions).

TEDDY BEAR WREATH

(Shown on page 35)

Your collection of teddy bears will turn an ordinary artificial evergreen wreath into a delightful accent this Christmas. Our 20" diameter wreath is the perfect size to hold a variety of teddy bears. First, we dressed our little friends in doll sweaters and hats and scarves made from torn fabric strips. Then we used florist wire to attach them to their temporary home. To add to the merriment, we used nylon thread to tie miniature snow shovels to the bears' paws and miniature sled ornaments to the wreath. One bear is even putting on a pair of doll-size skates! For snowballs, we applied craft glue to white pom-poms and rolled them in artificial snow. Straight pins hold some snowballs snugly in place in two playful bears' paws, while other snowballs are tucked among the branches of the wreath. Artificial snow is sprinkled over the entire wreath for a fresh, snowy look. For a final touch, we added a multi-loop bow at the bottom (see Multi-Loop Bow instructions).

SEASON'S GREETINGS WREATH (Shown on page 35)

Create this easy-to-assemble wreath in no time to welcome holiday guests. With a purchased bay leaf wreath, a hot glue gun, glue sticks, and an assortment of decorations that can be found at your local craft store, this wreath can be completed in minutes. Our decorations include dried pomegranates, stems of artificial berries, assorted pinecones, nuts, and sprigs of evergreen, which are all hot glued in place on the wreath. We used a black fabric marking pen with medium point to write our holiday messages on purchased wooden heart cutouts and then used a stencil brush to lightly stamp the edges of the hearts with brown paint to give them a natural finish. A raffia bow hot glued in place completes this cheerful wreath.

DOUBLE-LOOP AND MULTI-LOOP BOWS

For each bow, you will need ribbon and florist wire.

For double-loop bow, you will **also** need a hot glue gun and glue sticks.

DOUBLE-LOOP BOW

1. Cut 6" from ribbon for bow center; set aside.

2. For first streamer, measure desired length of streamer from 1 end of ribbon and gather ribbon between fingers (**Fig. 1**).

Fig. 1

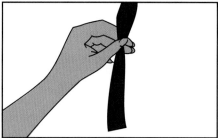

3. For first loop, keep right side facing out and fold ribbon over to form desired size loop (**Fig. 2**).

Fig. 2

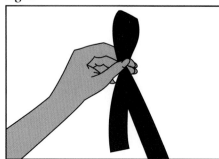

4. Repeat to form another loop same size as first loop (**Fig. 3**).

Fig. 3

5. Repeat Steps 3 and 4 to form 2 more loops.

6. To secure bow with wire, hold gathered loops tightly. Bring length of wire over and around center of bow. Hold wire behind bow center, gathering all loops forward; twist bow to tighten wire. Arrange loops as desired.

7. For bow center, loosely gather 6" length of ribbon lengthwise. With right side out, wrap gathered ribbon around center of bow, overlapping ends at back and trimming excess. Glue to secure.

8. Trim ribbon ends as desired.

MULTI-LOOP BOW

1. Follow Steps 2 - 5 of Double-Loop Bow instructions, repeating Step 5 until desired number of loops are made.

2. Follow Steps 6 and 8 of Double-Loop Bow instructions.

RUSTIC SANTA

Old Saint Nick is always a favorite character in holiday decorating, and this charming country image of him is perfect for indoors or out! Just paint his simple features on a fence board and use a wooden bead nose, raffia bow, and bell for the finishing touches. The jolly fellow is so much fun to make, you'll want to craft several more to share with friends.

FENCE POST SANTA

Fence post Santa is suitable for protected outdoor use, but should not be exposed to inclement weather.

You will need a 5¹⁄₂"w x 4'h fence board; a handsaw; white, peach, pink, red, brown, and black acrylic paint; black and iridescent glitter dimensional paint in squeeze bottles; Duncan Snow Accents™; a ⁷⁄₈" dia. wooden bead; a 1¹⁄₂" jingle bell; foam brushes; round paintbrushes; raffia; a drawing compass; soft cloth; hot glue gun; and glue sticks.

1. Referring to **Diagram**, use saw to cut top 4¹⁄₄" of board to a point. Use a pencil to draw lines on board as indicated in **Diagram**. Use compass to draw two 1¹⁄₄" dia. circles at center front of coat for buttons.

2. (**Note:** Refer to **Diagram** for painting; if desired, extend painted areas to sides and back of board. Allow to dry after each paint color.) Paint hat, coat, and pants red. Paint hat trim, mustache and beard, and cuffs white. Paint buttons, belt, and boots black. Paint face peach.

3. Apply Duncan Snow Accents™ to hat trim and cuffs.

4. Use iridescent glitter dimensional paint to outline hat trim, mustache, beard, and cuffs; to draw details on mustache and beard; and to paint a small "X" at center of each button to resemble stitches.

5. Use black dimensional paint to paint eyes, to outline buttons, to paint belt buckle at center of belt, and to paint over center line on pants and boots.

6. For cheeks, mix 1 part pink paint with 1 part water; use mixture to paint cheeks.

7. For nose, paint bead red; allow to dry. Glue bead to face.

8. To antique Santa, mix 1 part brown paint with 1 part water. Working on 1 small area at a time, use foam brush to apply mixture to Santa; quickly remove excess stain with soft cloth. Allow to dry.

9. Thread bell onto center of raffia and tie raffia into a bow. Glue bow to point of hat.

DIAGRAM

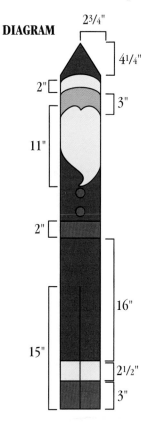

A Touch Of Victoriana

Our collection of nostalgic Santas makes it easy to bring the classic charm of a Victorian Christmas to your home. Filled with popular images from the turn of the century, these accents are also perfect for today's decor. The hand-tinted greeting cards and ornate decorations are highlighted by opulent textures and beautiful colors, but they don't require an elaborate effort to craft. Just build on purchased elements and follow our simplified techniques to create your own elegant celebration!

The rich fabrics and holiday hues of Victorian crazy quilts are a natural addition to Yuletide decorating. Our tree skirt allows you to enjoy the quilted look without sewing a stitch — simply fuse festive fabrics to a piece of muslin and use dimensional paint to add the "stitching"! (Opposite) *By photocopying and coloring a design you've selected, you can turn any black-and-white illustration into a customized Christmas card. Your loved ones will cherish the Victorian spirit of your handcrafted greetings.*

The custom of trimming an evergreen at Christmas became popular in England with the marriage of Queen Victoria to Prince Albert of Germany. Among those early tree trims, we might have found a lavishly decoupaged ornament such as the one shown here. It's crafted in minutes by painting a papier mâché ball and gluing on wrapping paper motifs and golden fringe.

Light up your celebration by embellishing fragrant candles with beautiful renderings of St. Nicholas. Just cut images of the gift-bringer from wrapping paper and use craft glue to smooth the cutouts onto pillar candles.

With photocopied designs and colored pencils, you can easily re-create the look of charming Victorian greeting cards. Choose a traditional verse for the inside, or pen your own wishes for a personalized holiday sentiment.

DECOUPAGED ORNAMENT

(Shown on page 40)

For each ornament, you will need a 4" dia. papier mâché ball, small motifs cut from wrapping paper, a 3/4" dia. wooden bead with a 3/8" dia. hole, 9" of 1/8" dia. gold twisted cord, 3" of 1" long gold fringe, desired color acrylic paint for ball, metallic gold acrylic paint for bead, small foam brushes, matte clear acrylic spray, craft glue, hot glue gun, and glue sticks.

1. (**Note:** Use a glass or cup with an opening slightly smaller than ball to hold ball while drying.) Allowing to dry between coats, apply 2 coats of paint to ball.
2. Mix 1 part craft glue with 1 part water. Use foam brush to apply a thin coat of mixture to back of 1 motif. Position motif on ball and smooth in place, working from center of motif outward (depending on size of motif, some wrinkling may occur along edges). Repeat to glue more motifs to ball until desired effect is achieved. Allow to dry.
3. Allowing to dry between coats, apply 2 coats of acrylic spray to ball.
4. For hanger, paint bead gold; allow to dry. Fold cord in half. Hot glue ends of cord into 1 end of bead. Hot glue bead to top of ball. Overlapping ends, hot glue fringe around bead.

DECORATED CANDLES

(Shown on page 40)

For each candle, you will need a pillar candle, motif cut from wrapping paper, foam brush, soft cloth, and craft glue.

Mix 1 part craft glue with 1 part water. Use foam brush to apply a thin coat of mixture to back of motif. Position motif on candle and smooth in place, working from center of motif outward. Use cloth to wipe away excess glue. Allow to dry.

CRAZY QUILT TREE SKIRT (Shown on page 39)

You will need a 44" square of muslin, fabric scraps to cover muslin, 1/2"w bias tape to coordinate with fabric scraps, 3 3/4 yds each of 1" long gold fringe and 1/4"w velvet ribbon, paper-backed fusible web, gold dimensional fabric paint in a squeeze bottle, fabric glue, removable fabric marking pen, string, and a thumbtack.

1. Follow manufacturer's instructions to fuse web to wrong sides of fabric scraps. Remove paper backing and arrange fabric scraps on muslin, trimming as desired to fit; fuse in place.
2. Matching right sides, fold muslin square in half from top to bottom and again from left to right.
3. To mark outer cutting line, tie 1 end of string to fabric marking pen. Insert thumbtack through string 20 1/2" from pen. Insert thumbtack in fabric as shown in **Fig. 1** and mark 1/4 of a circle.

Fig. 1

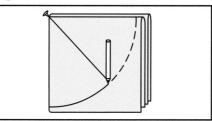

4. To mark inner cutting line, repeat Step 3, inserting thumbtack through string 1" from pen.
5. Cutting through all layers of fabric, cut out muslin along marked lines. For opening in back of skirt, cut through 1 layer of fabric along 1 fold line from outer to inner edge.
6. Lay skirt on a flat surface. Referring to photo, paint decorative "stitches" along raw edges of fabric scraps. Allow to dry.
7. For binding, insert opening edges and inner edge of skirt into fold of bias tape and glue to secure, trimming bias tape to fit.

8. Glue fringe along outer edge on right side of skirt, trimming to fit. Allow to dry.
9. With 1/2" of ribbon extending beyond 1 opening edge of skirt, glue ribbon along top edge of fringe; trim remaining ribbon end 1/2" from remaining opening edge of skirt. Fold ribbon ends to wrong side of skirt and glue in place.

CHRISTMAS CARDS AND ENVELOPES

(Shown on pages 38 and 41)

The illustrations we used for our cards (shown on pages 43 and 115) are from the Dover Clip-Art Series® "Old-fashioned Christmas Illustrations," but any black-and-white illustration can be used.

For each card and envelope, you will need heavyweight handmade paper for card, lightweight handmade paper for envelope, a black-and-white illustration for card, white copier paper, colored pencils, metallic gold paint pen with fine point (optional), Design Master® glossy wood tone spray (available at craft stores and florist shops), craft glue, spray adhesive, and double-sided tape.

1. To photocopy illustration by itself onto a piece of copier paper, photocopy illustration onto copier paper and cut out. Use spray adhesive to glue illustration to center of another piece of copier paper. Photocopy illustration again.
2. Use colored pencils to color copied illustration as desired.
3. Lightly spray colored illustration with wood tone spray. Allow to dry.
4. Leaving desired space around illustration, use a pencil and ruler to lightly draw a rectangle around illustration; cut out illustration just inside drawn lines.
5. Measure width of cutout; add 3/4" (for card with gold border) or 1/4" (for card

without gold border) and multiply by 2. Measure height of cutout; add ¾" (for card with gold border) or ¼" (for card without gold border). Cut a piece of heavyweight handmade paper the determined measurements. Match smooth sides and short edges and fold paper piece in half.

6. Use spray adhesive to glue illustration cutout to center front of card.

7. For card with gold border, use gold pen to draw a border along edge of cutout.

8. If desired, use gold pen to highlight details on colored illustration.

9. For envelope, measure width of card; multiply by 2 and add 3". Measure height of card; add 1". Cut a piece of lightweight handmade paper the determined measurements. Fold 1 short edge (flap) of paper 2" to 1 side; unfold. Fold remaining short edge to meet fold of flap; crease folds. Unfold paper and use craft glue to glue side edges together; allow to dry.

10. Write greeting in card and place card in envelope. Use tape to seal flap of envelope.

See page 115 for more card illustrations

GIFTS IN A JIFFY

*H*andmade gifts always touch the heart. No matter how simple, they reflect your love and carry with them a special feeling that will long be remembered. This year, you can wrap up your gift-giving in a jiffy with our quick-to-craft projects for everyone on your list. From festive clothing to holiday afghans, these gifts are all created using easy techniques and time-saving products. And because you make them yourself, they'll be treasured for years!

HEARTWARMING MUFFLER SET

GINGERBREAD WARMERS

*W*arm up a ready-made muffler set with friendly gingerbread men and heart appliqués. Attached with fusible web, the adorable motifs are trimmed with blanket stitching for a homey finishing touch. These toasty gifts will keep a country friend snug on those chilly winter afternoons.

You will need a cap, scarf, mittens, light brown felt for gingerbread men, fabric for hearts, brown embroidery floss and floss to coordinate with fabric, 1/8"w ribbon for bows, thread to match ribbon, paper-backed fusible web, and tracing paper.

1. Trace patterns onto tracing paper; cut out.

2. Follow manufacturer's instructions to fuse web to wrong sides of felt and fabric.

3. For cap, use pattern to cut 3 gingerbread men from felt. For scarf, use patterns to cut 1 gingerbread man from felt and 1 large heart from fabric. For mittens, use pattern to cut 2 small hearts from fabric.

4. Arrange appliqués on cap, scarf, and mittens; fuse in place.

5. Using brown floss for gingerbread men and coordinating floss for hearts, use 3 strands of floss to work **Blanket Stitch**, page 123, along edges of each appliqué. Use 12 strands of brown floss to work a **French Knot**, page 123, for each eye on gingerbread men.

6. For bow on each gingerbread man, tie a 7" length of ribbon into a bow; trim ends. Use matching thread to tack bow to gingerbread man.

POINSETTIA WRAP-UP

*W*rapped in our festive flowerpot cover, a brilliant poinsettia will be the perfect hostess gift for a holiday party. The cover is padded with batting for a poufed effect, gathered using a rubber band, and tied with a starry garland. Easy enough for beginning crafters, this no-sew gift is a fast and inexpensive way to spread holiday cheer!

PADDED POT COVER

For cover for flowerpot, you will need fabric, high-loft polyester bonded batting, gold wired star garland, masking tape, hot glue gun, glue sticks, and a large rubber band.

1. Measure pot from 1 side of rim to opposite side of rim (**Fig. 1**); add 8". Cut a circle of fabric the determined measurement.

Fig. 1

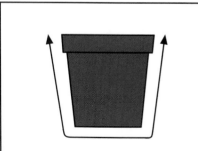

2. For padding, measure height of pot; subtract 1". Measure around sides of pot at widest point. Cut 2 strips of batting the determined measurements. With 1 long edge of each batting strip 1" below top edge of pot, glue batting strips around sides of pot.

3. Center pot on wrong side of fabric circle. Bring edges of circle to inside of pot and secure with tape. Place rubber band around fabric and pot 1" below top edge of pot. Remove tape and fold edges of fabric circle to wrong side, tucking edges under rubber band. If desired, use glue to secure fabric in place.

4. Wrap garland around pot, covering rubber band.

CHEERY CHRISTMAS TOWELS

These cute towels will bring holiday cheer to Mom's busy kitchen. The heart and tree shapes, cut from a variety of plaid and checked fabrics, are easily fused to ready-made towels and machine appliquéd using clear nylon thread. With these lasting gifts, your mother will have heartwarming thoughts of you for many Christmases to come.

COUNTRY KITCHEN TOWELS

For each towel, you will need a purchased towel, 2 fabrics for appliqués, 9" of ³/₈"w ribbon, paper-backed fusible web, tear-away stabilizer, fine clear nylon thread, thread to match towel, tracing paper, and a safety pin.

1. Wash and dry towel and fabrics several times to pre-shrink as much as possible; press.

2. Follow manufacturer's instructions to fuse web to wrong sides of appliqué fabrics. Do not remove paper backing.

3. Trace heart or tree pattern, page 116, onto tracing paper; cut out.

4. Use pattern to cut shape from 1 appliqué fabric. Remove paper backing and fuse shape to remaining appliqué fabric. Cutting approx. ¹/₄" outside shape, cut shape from second fabric. Remove paper backing and fuse shape to towel.

5. Position stabilizer on wrong side of towel behind appliqué; baste in place.

6. To machine appliqué, thread sewing machine with nylon thread in top and thread to match towel in bobbin. Using a medium width zigzag stitch with a short stitch length, test stitching on scrap fabric and adjust upper tension as necessary. Stitch over raw edges of appliqués. To finish, pull loose threads to wrong side of towel; knot and trim ends. Remove basting threads and stabilizer from towel.

7. Tie ribbon into a bow; trim ends. Using safety pin on wrong side of towel, pin bow to towel.

8. Remove bow before laundering.

PILLOW DRESSING

These holiday pillows couldn't be easier to craft using our fun no-sew techniques! The festive holly print cushion is created by wrapping fabric around a pillow and using a rubber band to secure the edges into a knot. For the others, you fashion slip-on pillow shams by fusing the seams. Ribbons and appliqués complete the dressy looks. As quick as these projects are, you'll have plenty of time to make them for lovely last-minute gifts.

WRAP PILLOW COVER

You will need a square pillow or pillow form, lightweight fabric to cover pillow, 2 strong rubber bands, safety pins, and 6"w decorative ribbon for bow.

1. To determine width of fabric piece, measure around pillow; add 8". To determine length of fabric piece, measure around pillow; add 12". Cut fabric the determined measurements.

2. Center pillow on wrong side of fabric. Fold long edges of fabric over pillow, overlapping at center; use safety pins to secure.

3. For knot, fold ends of fabric to center of pillow, gather ends together, and tightly wrap 1 rubber band around ends of fabric close to pillow (**Fig. 1**). Bring 1 outer layer of excess fabric (fabric above rubber band) over remaining excess fabric (**Fig. 2**); bring edges of outer layer of fabric around and under rubber band-secured fabric and use a safety pin to secure (**Fig. 2**).

Fig. 1

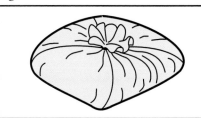

Fig. 2

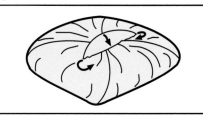

4. For bow, overlap ends of ribbon 2" and form desired-size loop. With overlap at center, flatten loop. Wrap remaining rubber band around center of loop to secure. Slip bow under knot on pillow cover and use a safety pin to secure.

RIBBON-TIED PILLOW COVER

You will need a pillow or pillow form, fabric to cover pillow, 1"w and 1/4"w paper-backed fusible web tape, 11/4"w ribbon, and fabric glue (optional).

1. Measure width of pillow; add 2". Measure height of pillow; double measurement and add 21/2". Cut fabric the determined measurements.

2. To hem opening edges of cover, follow manufacturer's instructions to fuse 1/4"w web tape along short edges on wrong side of fabric piece. Do not remove paper backing. Lightly press edges 1/4" to wrong side. Unfold edges and remove paper backing. Refold edges and fuse in place.

3. Fuse 1"w web tape along long edges on right side of fabric piece. Do not remove paper backing. Fold short edges of fabric piece to right side, overlapping 2" at center (**Fig. 1**); lightly press. Unfold edges and remove paper backing. Refold edges and fuse in place.

Fig. 1

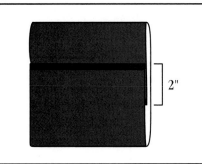

4. Turn pillow cover right side out and press; insert pillow. Wrap ribbon gift wrap-style around pillow and tie into a bow; trim ends. Use glue to secure ribbon if desired.

APPLIQUÉD PILLOW COVER

For a cover for a 15" square pillow, you will need a 17" fabric square for cover front, two 101/4" x 17" fabric pieces for cover back, two 35/8" x 17" fabric strips for trim strips, print fabric for appliqués, 1"w and 1/4"w paper-backed fusible web tape, paper-backed fusible web, and dimensional paint in squeeze bottle with fine tip to coordinate with appliqué fabric.

1. For each trim strip, follow manufacturer's instructions to fuse 1"w web tape along long edges on wrong side of fabric strip; do not remove paper backing. Lightly press long edges of strip 1" to wrong side. Unfold edges and remove paper backing. Refold edges and fuse in place. Fuse 1"w web tape along center on wrong side of strip. Remove paper backing.

2. For appliqués, follow manufacturer's instructions to fuse web to wrong side of appliqué fabric. Cut desired motifs from fabric. Remove paper backing.

3. Position trim strips and appliqués on cover front fabric square; fuse in place. Use paint to paint over raw edges and detail lines on appliqués; allow to dry.

4. To hem opening edges of cover back, fuse 1/4"w web tape along 1 long edge on wrong side of each 101/4" x 17" fabric piece. Do not remove paper backing. Lightly press edges 1/4" to wrong side. Unfold edges and remove paper backing. Refold edges and fuse in place.

5. To assemble cover, fuse 1"w web tape along each raw edge on right side of cover front fabric square and each cover back fabric piece; remove paper backing. With right sides together and matching raw edges, place cover back pieces on cover front square with hemmed edges of back pieces overlapping 3" at center. Fuse fabric pieces together.

6. Turn pillow cover right side out and press; insert pillow.

GLITZY SNEAKERS

A footloose teenager will step out in style with these glitzy decorated sneakers! They're easily made by adding glittery fabric paints, sequins, braid, and other trims to purchased canvas shoes. For added holiday flair, lace them up with flashy ribbons.

RED SEQUINED SNEAKERS

You will need a pair of white lace-up canvas sneakers, red glitter fabric paint, red string sequins, red metallic rickrack, 3/16"w red and gold metallic ribbon to replace laces, two 1/2" dia. gold jingle bells, fabric glue, small flat paintbrush, and tissue paper.

1. Remove laces from shoes and stuff shoes firmly with tissue paper.
2. Leaving bindings unpainted, paint canvas areas of shoes with red glitter paint. Allow to dry.
3. Glue rickrack along seam across top of each shoe, trimming to fit; allow to dry. Glue string sequins to shoes along top edges of soles, trimming to fit; allow to dry.
4. For laces, cut 2 ribbon lengths same length as laces. Thread 1 jingle bell onto each ribbon length; lace shoes with ribbons.

SNOWFLAKE SNEAKERS

You will need a pair of navy lace-up canvas sneakers, iridescent glitter fabric paint, small flat paintbrush, 12 white bugle beads, fourteen 5mm pearl beads, 7/8"w plaid ribbon to replace laces, jewel glue, and tissue paper.

1. Follow Step 1 of Red Sequined Sneakers.
2. Leaving bindings unpainted, paint canvas areas of shoes with iridescent glitter paint. Allow to dry.
3. For snowflakes, glue 6 bugle beads and 7 pearl beads to toe of each shoe. Allow to dry.
4. For laces, cut 2 ribbon lengths same length as laces; lace shoes with ribbons.

GREEN PLAID SNEAKERS

You will need a pair of green lace-up canvas sneakers, gold glitter fabric paint, 1/4"w flat paintbrush, 3/16" dia. multi-colored metallic cord, 5/8"w gold mesh

ribbon to replace laces, 2 silk holly sprigs, tissue paper, fabric glue, hot glue gun, and glue sticks.

1. Follow Step 1 of Red Sequined Sneakers.
2. Leaving bindings unpainted, use gold glitter paint to paint horizontal and vertical lines approx. 1/2" apart on canvas areas of shoes to form a grid. Allow to dry.
3. Use fabric glue to glue cord to shoes along top edges of soles, trimming to fit; allow to dry.
4. For laces, cut 2 ribbon lengths same length as laces; lace shoes with ribbons.
5. Hot glue 1 holly sprig to each shoe.

PRETTY POINSETTIA APRON

*I*t's fun to "season" a gourmet's Christmas cooking with this pretty poinsettia apron! Appliquéd using an easy no-sew technique, silk poinsettias and festive fabrics are transformed into a wearable pot of cheer. Golden fabric paints and a plaid bow provide glittery finishing touches.

PRETTY POINSETTIA APRON

You will need a white apron, red and gold silk poinsettias, silk holly leaves, fabric for pot, 1/2 yd of 1 1/2"w ribbon, green and gold fabric paint, small flat paintbrush, textile medium, gold dimensional paint in squeeze bottle, old toothbrush, paper-backed fusible web, tracing paper, scrap paper, safety pin, and aluminum foil.

1. Wash, dry, and press apron according to fabric paint manufacturer's recommendations.

2. For pot, use pot pattern, page 115, and follow **Tracing Patterns**, page 123. Follow manufacturer's instructions to fuse web to wrong side of fabric. Use pattern to cut pot from fabric. For pot rim, cut a 1 1/8" x 5 1/2" strip of fabric.

3. Position pot at center front of apron approx. 7 1/2" from top edge; fuse in place. Overlapping top of pot slightly, center and fuse pot rim to apron above pot.

4. Remove petal sections from poinsettia stems, discarding any plastic or metal pieces; repeat for holly leaves. Test petals and leaves for washability by hand washing 1 petal section and 1 leaf. Do not use petal sections or leaves that are not colorfast.

5. Use warm, dry iron to press 2 red petal

sections, 2 gold petal sections, and 3 holly leaves.

6. Place a large piece of aluminum foil shiny side up on ironing board. Place petal sections and leaves wrong side up on foil. Cover flowers and leaves with a piece of web. Fuse web to wrong sides of flowers and leaves. Allow to cool. Remove paper backing. Peel flowers and leaves from foil and trim excess web from edges.

7. Arrange flowers and leaves on apron and fuse in place.

8. Lightly brush gold fabric paint on red petals and holly leaves; allow to dry.

9. Use gold dimensional paint to paint over raw edges of pot and pot rim and to paint dots at centers of poinsettias. Allow to dry.

10. (**Note:** Practice spattering technique on scrap paper before painting apron.) To make a mask for appliqué design, cut a piece of scrap paper slightly larger than design; place paper over appliqués. To spatter-paint apron, mix 1 part green paint with 1 part textile medium. Dip toothbrush in mixture and pull thumb firmly across bristles to spatter paint onto apron. Repeat as desired. Allow to dry and remove scrap paper.

11. Tie ribbon into a bow; trim ends. Using safety pin on wrong side of apron, pin bow to apron.

12. Remove bow before laundering. Follow web and paint manufacturers' recommendations for laundering.

*L*ight up a friend's holiday with these festive candle holders crafted from "recycled" food cans. Just dress them up with paint and then embellish a wreath with sweet miniatures, trim a tiny tree with colorful buttons, or add a smiling snowman in wintry white. Present the cans with scented votive candles and these little lights will fill the house with Yuletide aroma.

WINTRY CANDLE TINS

For each tin, you will need a small can (we used 8-ounce tomato sauce cans), spray primer, and white vinegar.

For tree tin, you will **also** need dark red spray paint, 1 small square each of poster board and green print fabric, three red buttons, 1 brown button, string, paper-backed fusible web, tracing paper, hot glue gun, and glue sticks.

For snowman tin, you will **also** need dark blue and white spray paint; white, pink, red, orange, brown, dark grey, and black acrylic paint; small and medium paintbrushes; tracing paper; and graphite transfer paper.

For wreath tin, you will **also** need ivory spray paint; miniature greenery garland, candy canes, and lollipops; several red buttons; string; hot glue gun; and glue sticks.

TREE TIN

1. Wash can in hot soapy water (do not use lemon-scented soap); rinse well. Rinse can in a solution of 1 part vinegar and 1 part water.
2. Allowing to dry between coats, spray can with several coats of primer.
3. Spray paint can dark red. Allow to dry.
4. Follow manufacturer's instructions to fuse web to wrong side of fabric square. Fuse fabric square to poster board square.
5. Trace tree pattern onto tracing paper; cut out. Use pattern to cut tree from fabric-covered poster board.
6. Glue tree to can. Glue red buttons to tree. Glue brown button below tree for trunk. Tie string into a bow around can; trim ends.

SNOWMAN TIN

1. Follow Steps 1 and 2 of Tree Tin instructions.
2. (**Note:** Allow to dry after each paint color.) Spray paint can dark blue.
3. Trace snowman pattern onto tracing paper. Use transfer paper to transfer pattern to can as desired. (We transferred pattern 3 times around can.)
4. (**Note:** Follow Steps 4 and 5 to paint each snowman.) Using medium paintbrush and white paint, use a stamping motion to paint body and scarf of snowman white. Using dark grey paint, repeat to paint hat.
5. (**Note:** Refer to photo and use small paintbrushes to paint details on each snowman.) Use red paint to paint plaid design and fringe on scarf. Use black paint to paint eyes, mouth, and buttons. Use orange paint to paint nose. Use pink paint to paint cheeks. Use brown paint to paint arms.
6. Apply a very light coat of white spray paint to can to resemble snow. Use tip of a paintbrush handle and white acrylic paint to paint dots on can for snowflakes. Allow to dry.

WREATH TIN

1. Follow Steps 1 and 2 of Tree Tin instructions.
2. Spray paint can ivory. Allow to dry.
3. For wreath, form miniature garland into an approx. 2$^1/_2$" dia. circle.
4. Glue candy canes, lollipops, and buttons to wreath. Tie string into a bow and glue to wreath. Glue wreath to can.

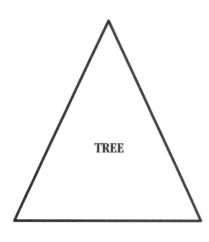

TREE

55

CAROLER'S SWEATSHIRT

*T*he caroler on your
gift list will sing glad tidings
when she dons this candle-
motif sweatshirt! The tapers
are cut from rich holiday
fabrics, fused in place, and
finished with a machine
appliqué edging. On a chilly
evening of caroling, this
sweatshirt will "light" her
path while she keeps cozy in
its fleecy warmth.

CHRISTMAS CANDLES SWEATSHIRT

You will need a sweatshirt, fabrics for candle and flame appliqués, thread to match fabrics, paper-backed fusible web, tear-away stabilizer, and tracing paper.

1. Wash, dry, and press shirt and fabrics.
2. For patterns, draw a 2¹/₄" x 8¹/₂" rectangle for small candle, a 2¹/₄" x 10¹/₂" rectangle for medium candle, and a 2¹/₄" x 13¹/₂" rectangle for large candle on tracing paper. Trace flame pattern onto tracing paper. Cut out patterns.
3. Follow manufacturer's instructions to fuse web to wrong sides of fabrics.
4. Use candle patterns to cut 2 small, 2 medium, and 1 large candle from fabrics. Use flame pattern to cut 5 flames from fabric.
5. Remove paper backing and arrange candles and flames on shirt; fuse in place.
6. Baste stabilizer to wrong side of shirt under appliqués.
7. Use matching thread and a medium width zigzag stitch with a very short stitch length to stitch over edges of appliqués.
8. Remove basting threads and stabilizer.

56

ABC BUTTON COVERS

*A*pples for your child's favorite teacher to wear will make an appealing gift this Christmas. Our easy-to-make button covers are crafted from colored paper, then finished with clear gloss and dimensional paint letters. Presented on a cleverly shaped card, these fashion accents will be enjoyed all through the school year.

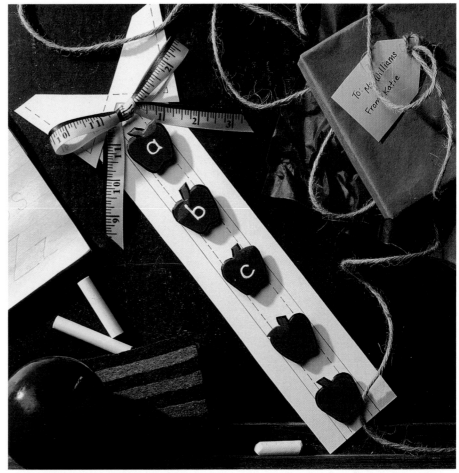

SHINY APPLE BUTTON COVERS

For button covers, you will need button cover hardware for each button cover; red, green, brown, and black paper; white poster board; white dimensional paint in squeeze bottle; Clear Clear Cote (clear gloss finish for paper crafts; available at craft stores); small paintbrush; drawing compass; tracing paper; craft glue; hot glue gun; and glue sticks.

For gift card, you will **also** need 20" of 5/8"w "ruler" ribbon, a black felt-tip pen with fine point, and double-sided transparent tape.

1. Trace apple, stem, and leaf patterns, page 114, onto tracing paper; cut out. Cutting 1 of each shape for each button cover, use patterns to cut apples from red paper, stems from brown paper, and leaves from green paper.

2. (**Note:** Use craft glue for all gluing unless otherwise indicated. Allow to dry after each glue step.) For each apple, position stem as desired and glue bottom of stem to wrong side of apple; glue leaf to apple. Glue apple to black paper. Trim black paper to 1/16" from edges of apple and stem and even with edges of leaf.

3. Use compass to draw a 1" dia. circle on poster board for each button cover; cut out. Glue 1 circle to back of each apple.

4. Use paintbrush to apply a thick coat of Clear Clear Cote to apples, being sure to bring coating to edges. Allow to dry 1 to 2 days.

5. Use white paint to paint letters on apples as desired; allow to dry.

6. Hot glue button cover hardware to back of each apple.

7. For gift card, trace collar pattern, page 114, onto tracing paper; cut out. Use pattern to cut collar from poster board. Cut a 2½" x 11¾" strip from poster board. Use pen and a ruler to draw dashed lines ¼" from edges of collar points to resemble stitching. Use pen and ruler to draw a solid line 5/8" from each long edge of poster board strip; draw a dashed line 7/8" from each long edge to resemble stitching. Overlapping collar over 1 end of strip, glue collar to strip. Tie ribbon into a bow; trim ends. Glue bow to gift card. Use tape to attach button covers to gift card.

*G*ive new meaning to the term stocking stuffers when you deliver our festive footwear for Christmas! Each pair of socks sports a cheerful symbol of the season cross stitched on the cuff. Great for last-minute gift ideas, these socks will help you foot the holiday bill.

FESTIVE SOCKS

For each pair of socks, you will need socks, one 3" square each of 14 mesh waste canvas and lightweight non-fusible interfacing for each design, sewing thread, embroidery floss (see color key), masking tape, tweezers, and spray bottle filled with water.

1. Cover edges of canvas with tape.

2. Find desired stitching area on sock and mark center of area with a pin. Use blue threads in canvas to place canvas straight on sock; pin canvas to sock. Pin interfacing to wrong side of sock under canvas. Basting through all layers, baste around edges of canvas, from corner to corner, and from side to side.

3. Using a sharp needle and 3 strands of floss for Cross Stitch and 1 for Backstitch and French Knots, work design, stitching from large holes to large holes.

4. Remove basting threads and trim canvas to within ³/₄" of design. Dampen canvas until it becomes limp. Use tweezers to pull out canvas threads one at a time. Trim interfacing close to design.

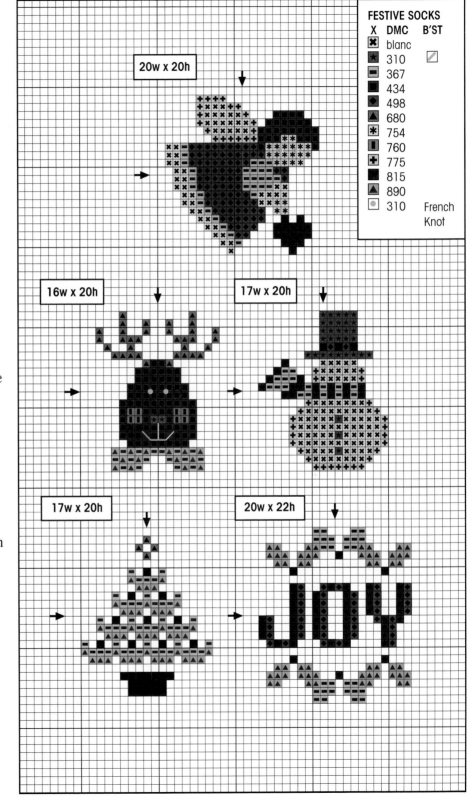

FESTIVE SOCKS		
X	DMC	B'ST
✖	blanc	
★	310	◿
⊟	367	
■	434	
◆	498	
▲	680	
✳	754	
▯	760	
✚	775	
■	815	
▲	890	
●	310	French Knot

20w x 20h

16w x 20h

17w x 20h

17w x 20h

20w x 22h

YULETIDE FRAMES

*F*estive fabrics and
shiny trims make these
covered picture frames an
endearing way to show off
photographs of loved ones.
You can surprise a proud
grandma or a dear friend
with a recent snapshot
tucked inside one of the
elegant holders. They're so
simple to craft, you can easily
make several in one evening!

PADDED CHRISTMAS FRAME

For frame to hold a 3½" x 5" photo,
you will need the following pieces of heavy
(corrugated) cardboard: one 5" x 6½"
piece each for frame front and frame back
and a 2" x 6" piece for frame stand; the
following pieces of fabric: a 7" x 8½" piece
to cover frame front, a 7" x 15" piece to
cover frame back, and a 4" x 14" piece to
cover frame stand; low-loft polyester
bonded batting; 1½ yds of ¼" dia. gold
twisted cord; fabric marking pencil; craft
knife; tracing paper; fabric glue; spray
adhesive; hot glue gun; and glue sticks.

1. For opening in frame front, trace oval
pattern onto tracing paper; cut out. Draw
around pattern at center of one 5" x 6½"
cardboard piece (frame front); use craft
knife to cut out opening.

2. To pad frame front, use frame front as a
pattern to cut a piece of batting. Use spray
adhesive to glue batting to 1 side of frame
front.

3. Center frame front on wrong side of
7" x 8½" fabric piece and use fabric
marking pencil to draw around opening;
remove frame front. Referring to **Fig. 1**, cut
fabric piece from center top to center
bottom of oval ¼" from drawn line; at ½"
intervals, clip fabric to ¼" from drawn line.

Fig. 1

4. (**Note:** Unless otherwise indicated, use hot glue for remaining steps.) Center frame front batting side down on wrong side of fabric piece. Alternating sides, fold clipped fabric edges over edge of opening to back of frame front; glue in place. Fold fabric corners diagonally over corners of frame front; glue in place (**Fig. 2**). Fold remaining fabric edges to back of frame front, pulling fabric until smooth; glue in place.

Fig. 2

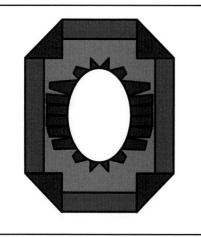

5. (**Note:** To prevent ends of cord from fraying after cutting, apply fabric glue to 1/2" around area to be cut, allow to dry, and then cut.) Hot glue a length of cord along edge of frame front, trimming to fit. Beginning and ending at bottom right of opening, repeat for frame front opening. Cut a 12" length of cord and tie into a bow; trim and fray ends. Glue bow to frame front, covering ends of cord around opening.

6. For frame back, apply spray adhesive to 1 side of remaining 5" x 6 1/2" cardboard piece (frame back). Place frame back adhesive side down on wrong side of 7" x 15 1/4" fabric piece and press in place (**Fig. 3**). Fold side edges of fabric to wrong side along side edges of frame back and hot glue in place. Fold bottom edge of fabric over frame back and glue in place. Fold top edge of fabric 1" to wrong side and glue in

place. Fold top half of fabric over frame back and glue along edges to secure.

Fig. 3

7. Glue side and bottom edges of frame back to back of frame front, leaving an opening at top for inserting photo.
8. For frame stand, use remaining cardboard and fabric pieces and repeat Step 6. Fold top 1 1/2" of frame stand to 1 side (right side). With frame stand centered on back of frame and bottom of frame stand even with bottom of frame, hot glue area of frame stand above fold to back of frame.

CHRISTMAS BOX FRAME

You will need an 8" x 10" x 1 1/2" plastic box frame with cardboard insert, fabric to cover insert, 1/2"w gimp trim, 1/4"w flat trim, 7/8"w satin ribbon, spray adhesive, fabric marking pencil, hot glue gun, glue sticks, and desired photo (5" x 7" or smaller).

1. Remove cardboard insert from frame.
2. To cover insert, use fabric marking pencil to draw around insert on wrong side of fabric. Cut out fabric 1 1/2" outside drawn

lines. Make a diagonal clip at each corner of fabric from corner to 1/4" from drawn line (**Fig. 1**).

Fig. 1

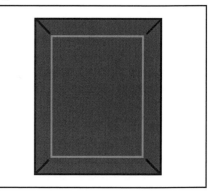

3. Apply spray adhesive to front and sides of insert and reposition insert front side down on wrong side of fabric. Referring to **Fig. 2**, press long edges of fabric onto sides of insert; press clipped ends around corners of insert onto short sides. At each short edge of fabric, use small dots of hot glue to glue clipped ends of short edges to wrong side (**Fig. 2**); press short edges of fabric onto sides of insert, using small dots of glue to glue ends in place.

Fig. 2

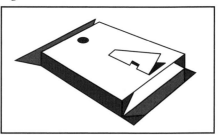

4. Making sure that hanger on back of insert is at top, use spray adhesive to glue photo to center front of insert. Place insert in frame.
5. Beginning at center top of photo, hot glue gimp trim to frame, covering edges of photo. Hot glue flat trim over gimp trim.
6. Tie ribbon into a bow; trim ends. Hot glue bow over ends of trims. Use small dots of hot glue to tack streamers in place.

ELEGANT AFGHAN

*C*rocheted in rich
Christmas red, this cozy
afghan will be a cherished
comforter throughout
the year. Its elegant spider
diamond pattern is made
quickly using simple stitches
worked with two strands of
yarn held together. To finish
the afghan, simply join the
panels, add the pretty edging,
and present it with your
warmest holiday wishes!

DOUBLE-STRAND DIAMOND AFGHAN

GENERAL INSTRUCTIONS
ABBREVIATIONS

ch(s)	chain(s)
dc	double crochet(s)
hdc	half double crochet(s)
mm	millimeters
sc	single crochet(s)
sp(s)	space(s)
st(s)	stitch(es)
YO	yarn over

★ — work instructions following ★ as many **more** times as indicated in addition to the first time.

† to † — work all instructions from first † to second † **as many** times as indicated.

( ) — contains explanatory remarks.

Note: To work Single Crochet, see **Fig. 7**, page 28; to work Double Crochet, see **Figs. 8** and **9**, page 29.

HALF DOUBLE CROCHET

YO, insert hook in st or sp indicated, YO and pull up a loop, YO and draw through all 3 loops on hook (**Fig. 1**).

Fig. 1

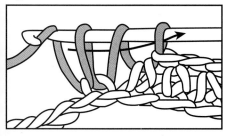

MATERIALS

Worsted Weight Yarn, approximately:
  60 ounces, (1,700 grams, 3,775 yards)
Crochet hook, size N (10.00 mm) **or** size needed for gauge
Yarn needle

INSTRUCTIONS

Finished Size: Approximately 52" x 62"

GAUGE: Working double strand in pattern, 10 dc and 6 rows = 4"
  Panel = 16½"
  DO NOT HESITATE TO CHANGE HOOK SIZE TO OBTAIN CORRECT GAUGE.

Note: Entire Afghan is worked holding two strands of yarn together.

PANEL (Make 3)
Ch 43 **loosely**.

Row 1 (Right side): Dc in fourth ch from hook and in next 18 chs, ch 1, skip next ch, dc in last 20 chs: 41 sts.

Note: Loop a short piece of yarn around any stitch to mark last row as **right** side and **top** edge.

Row 2: Ch 3 (**counts as first dc, now and throughout**), turn; dc in next 17 dc, ch 1, skip next dc, dc in next dc, dc in next ch-1 sp and in next dc, ch 1, skip next dc, dc in last 18 dc: 39 dc.

Row 3: Ch 3, turn; dc in next 15 dc, ch 1, ★ skip next dc, dc in next dc, dc in next ch-1 sp and in next dc, ch 1; repeat from ★ once **more**, skip next dc, dc in last 16 dc: 38 dc.

Row 4: Ch 3, turn; dc in next 13 dc, ch 1, skip next dc, dc in next dc, dc in next ch-1 sp and in next dc, ch 2, skip next 2 dc, dc in next ch-1 sp, ch 2, skip next 2 dc, dc in next dc, dc in next ch-1 sp and in next dc, ch 1, skip next dc, dc in last 14 dc: 35 dc.

Row 5: Ch 3, turn; dc in next 11 dc, ch 1, skip next dc, dc in next dc, dc in next ch-1 sp and in next dc, ch 3, skip next 2 dc, sc in next ch-2 sp and in next dc, sc in next ch-2 sp, ch 3, skip next 2 dc, dc in next dc, dc in next ch-1 sp and in next dc, ch 1, skip next dc, dc in last 12 dc: 30 dc.

Row 6: Ch 3, turn; dc in next 9 dc, ch 1, skip next dc, dc in next dc, dc in next ch-1 sp and in next dc, ch 3, skip next 2 dc, sc in next ch-3 sp, sc in next 3 sc and in next ch-3 sp, ch 3, skip next 2 dc, dc in next dc, dc in next ch-1 sp and in next dc, ch 1, skip next dc, dc in last 10 dc: 26 dc.

Row 7: Ch 3, turn; dc in next 7 dc, ch 1, skip next dc, dc in next dc, dc in next ch-1 sp and in next dc, ch 3, skip next dc, dc in next dc, 2 dc in next ch-3 sp, ch 4, skip next sc, sc in next 3 sc, ch 4, skip next sc, 2 dc in next ch-3 sp, dc in next dc, ch 3, skip next dc, dc in next dc, dc in next ch-1 sp and in next dc, ch 1, skip next dc, dc in last 8 dc: 28 dc.

Row 8: Ch 3, turn; dc in next 5 dc, ch 1, skip next dc, dc in next dc and in next ch-1 sp, † dc in next dc, ch 4, skip next 2 dc, dc in next ch-3 sp, ch 4, skip next 2 dc, dc in next dc †, 2 dc in next ch-4 sp, ch 4, skip next sc, dc in next sc, ch 4, skip next sc, 2 dc in next ch-4 sp, repeat from † to † once, dc in next ch-1 sp and in next dc, ch 1, skip next dc, dc in last 6 dc: 27 dc.

Row 9: Ch 3, turn; dc in next 3 dc, ch 1, skip next dc, dc in next dc and in next ch-1 sp, † dc in next dc, ch 5, skip next 2 dc, sc in next ch-4 sp and in next dc, sc in next ch-4 sp, ch 5, skip next 2 dc, dc in next dc †, 2 dc in next ch-4 sp, ch 5, skip next dc, 2 dc in next ch-4 sp, repeat from † to † once, dc in next ch-1 sp and in next dc, ch 1, skip next dc, dc in last 4 dc: 20 dc.

Row 10: Ch 3, turn; dc in next dc, ch 1, skip next dc, dc in next dc and in next ch-1 sp, † dc in next dc, ch 5, skip next 2 dc, sc in next loop and in next 3 sc, sc in next loop, ch 5, skip next 2 dc, dc in next dc †, dc in next loop, repeat from † to † once, dc in next ch-1 sp and in next dc, ch 1, skip next dc, dc in last 2 dc: 13 dc.

Continued on page 64

DOUBLE-STRAND DIAMOND AFGHAN (continued)

Row 11: Ch 3, turn; dc in next dc and in next ch-1 sp, dc in next dc, ch 1, † skip next dc, dc in next dc, 2 dc in next loop, ch 5, skip next sc, sc in next 3 sc, ch 5, skip next sc, 2 dc in next loop, dc in next dc †, ch 5, repeat from † to † once, ch 1, skip next dc, dc in next dc, dc in next ch-1 sp and in last 2 dc: 20 dc.

Row 12: Ch 3, turn; dc in next 3 dc, dc in next ch-1 sp and in next dc, ch 1, skip next dc, † dc in next dc, 2 dc in next loop, ch 4, skip next sc, dc in next sc, ch 4, skip next sc, 2 dc in next loop, dc in next dc †, ch 4, skip next 2 dc, dc in next loop, ch 4, skip next 2 dc, repeat from † to † once, ch 1, skip next dc, dc in next dc, dc in next ch-1 sp and in last 4 dc: 27 dc.

Row 13: Ch 3, turn; dc in next 5 dc, dc in next ch-1 sp and in next dc, ch 1, skip next dc, † dc in next dc, 2 dc in next ch-4 sp, ch 2, skip next dc, 2 dc in next ch-4 sp, dc in next dc †, ch 3, skip next 2 dc, sc in next ch-4 sp and in next dc, sc in next ch-4 sp, ch 3, skip next 2 dc, repeat from † to † once, ch 1, skip next dc, dc in next dc, dc in next ch-1 sp and in last 6 dc: 28 dc.

Row 14: Ch 3, turn; dc in next 7 dc, dc in next ch-1 sp and in next dc, ch 1, skip next dc, dc in next dc, dc in next ch-2 sp and in next dc, ch 3, skip next 2 dc, sc in next ch-3 sp and in next 3 sc, sc in next ch-3 sp, ch 3, skip next 2 dc, dc in next dc, dc in next ch-2 sp and in next dc, ch 1, skip next dc, dc in next dc, dc in next ch-1 sp and in last 8 dc: 26 dc.

Row 15: Ch 3, turn; dc in next 9 dc, dc in next ch-1 sp and in next dc, ch 1, skip next dc, dc in next dc, 2 dc in next ch-3 sp, ch 3, skip next sc, sc in next 3 sc, ch 3, skip next sc, 2 dc in next ch-3 sp, dc in next dc, ch 1, skip next dc, dc in next dc, dc in next ch-1 sp and in last 10 dc: 30 dc.

Row 16: Ch 3, turn; dc in next 11 dc, dc in next ch-1 sp and in next dc, ch 1, skip next dc, dc in next dc, 2 dc in next ch-3 sp, ch 2, skip next sc, sc in next sc, ch 2, skip next sc, 2 dc in next ch-3 sp, dc in next dc, ch 1, skip next dc, dc in next dc, dc in next ch-1 sp and in last 12 dc: 35 dc.

Row 17: Ch 3, turn; dc in next 13 dc, dc in next ch-1 sp and in next dc, ch 1, skip next dc, dc in next dc, 2 dc in next ch-2 sp, ch 1, skip next dc, 2 dc in next ch-2 sp, dc in next dc, ch 1, skip next dc, dc in next dc, dc in next ch-1 sp and in last 14 dc: 38 dc.

Row 18: Ch 3, turn; dc in next 15 dc, ★ dc in next ch-1 sp and in next dc, ch 1, skip next dc, dc in next dc; repeat from ★ once **more**, dc in next ch-1 sp and in last 16 dc: 39 dc.

Row 19: Ch 3, turn; dc in next 17 dc, dc in next ch-1 sp and in next dc, ch 1, skip next dc, dc in next dc, dc in next ch-1 sp and in last 18 dc: 40 dc.

Rows 20-91: Repeat Rows 2-19, 4 times; do **not** finish off.

PANEL EDGING

Ch 1, do **not** turn; work 152 sc evenly spaced across ends of rows; working in free loops of beginning ch (**Fig. 5, page 28**), 3 sc in first ch, sc in each ch across to last ch, 3 sc in last ch; work 152 sc evenly spaced across ends of rows; 3 sc in first dc, sc in each dc and in ch-1 sp across to last dc, 3 sc in last dc; join with slip st to first sc, finish off: 394 sc.

ASSEMBLY

Weave Panels together as follows: Place two Panels with **right** sides together and marked edges at top. Beginning in corner sc, sew through both pieces once to secure the beginning of the seam, leaving an ample yarn end to weave in later. Working through inside loops of each stitch of both Panels, insert the needle from **back** to **front** through first stitch and pull yarn through (**Fig. 10, page 29**), ★ insert needle from **back** to **front** through **next** stitch and pull yarn through; repeat from ★ across.

EDGING

With **right** side facing, join yarn with slip st in upper right corner; ch 1, hdc in same st, ch 1; working from **left** to **right**, skip next sc, ★ YO, insert hook in next sc (**Fig. 2**), YO and draw through, under and to left of loops on hook (3 loops on hook) (**Fig. 3**), YO and draw through all 3 loops on hook (**Fig. 4**) (**Reverse hdc made, Fig. 5**), ch 1, skip next sc; repeat from ★ around; join with slip st to first st, finish off.

Fig. 2   **Fig. 3**

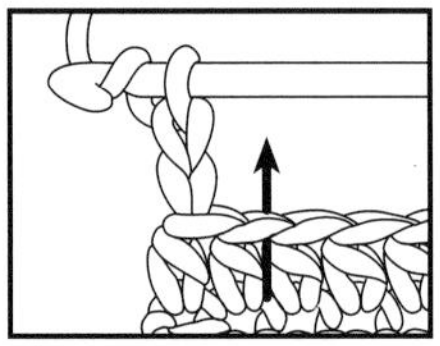

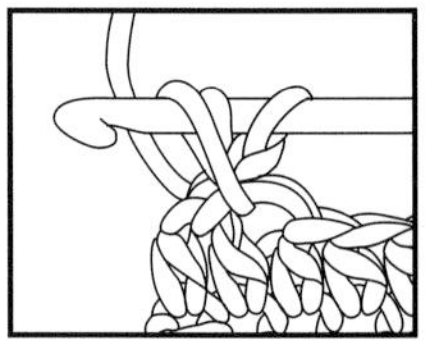

Fig. 4 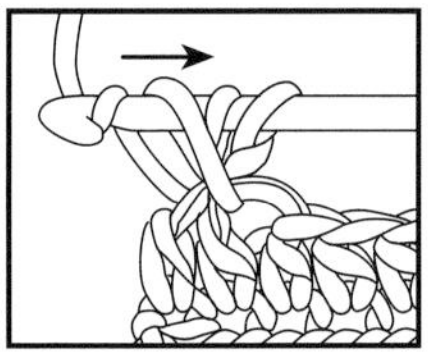   **Fig. 5**

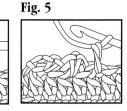

CHRISTMAS PAPER ART

*C*ast your warmest
holiday wishes into a
delightful pin or decoration
using pre-mixed papier
mâché and your favorite
candy or cookie mold.
Painted with a wash of festive
colors and presented early,
these gifts will bring cheer
throughout the season.

CHRISTMAS PAPER ART

For each shape, you will need a plastic, metal, or clay mold; Creative Paperclay™ (available at craft stores); a white paper towel; matte clear acrylic spray; desired colors of acrylic paint; paintbrushes; colored charcoal paper for backing; hot glue gun; glue sticks; Design Master® glossy wood tone spray (optional; available at craft stores and florist shops); and items to decorate shape (optional; we used a bow tied from 1/4"w satin ribbon).
For framed shape, you will **also** need a frame to fit shape, fabric for background, poster board, and paper-backed fusible web.
For pin, you will **also** need a pin back.

1. Wet paper towel and lay over mold. Firmly press Creative Paperclay™ into mold, allowing clay to extend beyond edges of mold.
2. If using a plastic mold, allow shape to dry in mold approx. 24 hours. If using a metal or clay mold, preheat oven to 350 degrees. Place mold on cookie sheet in oven; immediately turn off oven and close door. After 20 minutes, remove mold from oven and allow to cool.

3. Gently remove shape from mold and allow to dry completely on a flat surface.
4. Allowing to dry between coats, apply 2 coats of acrylic spray to shape.
5. Dilute each color of paint by adding 2 parts water to 1 part paint. Paint shape with diluted paint; allow to dry.
6. Repeat Step 4.
7. For backing, tear a piece from charcoal paper 1" larger on all sides than shape. Glue edges of shape to paper. Tear excess charcoal paper to approx. 1/4" from edges of shape.

8. To antique shape, lightly spray shape with wood tone spray if desired; allow to dry.
9. If desired, glue decorative items to shape.
10. For framed paper shape, follow manufacturer's instructions to fuse web to wrong side of fabric. Fuse fabric to poster board. Cut fabric-covered poster board to fit frame. Glue shape to center of poster board and place poster board in frame.
11. For pin, glue pin back to back of shape.

SNOWY "IN-VEST-MENT"

*F**ull of wintry cheer, this whimsical snowman won't melt away when he comes in from the cold! He's cleverly crafted by fusing simple fabric shapes onto a purchased denim vest. Finished with a few easy details, our playful vest will delight a fun-loving friend.*

EASY APPLIQUÉD VEST

You will need a vest, fabrics for appliqués, a 1¼" x 7" fabric strip for scarf, paper-backed fusible web, a 1" dia. white pom-pom, white thread, small safety pin, seam ripper, black permanent felt-tip pen with medium point, and buttons and coordinating thread to replace buttons on vest (optional).

1. Wash, dry, and press vest and appliqué fabrics.

2. If necessary, use seam ripper to remove false pocket from left side of vest.

3. Leaving approx. 1" around each pattern, trace patterns, page 117, onto paper side of web. Leaving approx. ½" around each shape, cut shapes from web.

4. Follow manufacturer's instructions to fuse web shapes to wrong sides of fabrics; cut out shapes along drawn lines.

5. Remove paper backing from shapes. Arrange shapes on vest and fuse in place.

6. Use black pen to outline shapes, to draw eye and mouth, and to draw line for trunk from tree to snowman's hand.

7. Tack pom-pom to point of hat.

8. For scarf, knot center of fabric strip; fray ends. Use safety pin on wrong side of vest to pin scarf to snowman.

9. If desired, replace buttons on vest.

10. Remove scarf before laundering. Follow web manufacturer's recommendations for laundering.

CANDLELIGHT PLACE MATS

It's easy to perk up ready-made place mats with these simple patterns! Just use colorful fabric paints to create the festive candles and holly. Add details with dimensional paints, then sprinkle the designs with colored glitter. Trimmed with lengths of gold braid, a set of these place mats is sure to delight a friend who enjoys holiday entertaining.

CANDLELIGHT PLACE MATS

For each place mat, you will need a purchased fringed place mat; 3/8"w flat gold braid trim; small flat paintbrushes; red, green, and gold fabric paint; red, green, gold, and gold glitter dimensional fabric paint in squeeze bottles with fine tips; red, green, and gold fine glitter; tracing paper; graphite transfer paper; and fabric glue.

1. Trace candle and holly patterns, page 119, onto tracing paper. With designs 3/4" from top and bottom edges of place mat, use transfer paper to transfer designs to place mat.

2. Allowing to dry after each color, use fabric paint to paint candles red, leaves green, and flames gold.

3. Use red dimensional paint to outline candles and to paint dots for berries. Before paint dries, sprinkle with red glitter; allow to dry and gently shake off excess glitter.

4. Use green dimensional paint to outline leaves and to paint veins on leaves. Before paint dries, sprinkle with green glitter; allow to dry and gently shake off excess glitter.

5. Use gold glitter dimensional paint to paint wicks and outline flames. Allow to dry.

6. Use gold dimensional paint to paint circles around flames. Before paint dries, sprinkle with gold glitter; allow to dry and gently shake off excess glitter.

7. (**Note:** To prevent ends of trim from fraying after cutting, apply fabric glue to 1/2" around area to be cut, allow to dry, and then cut.) Measure length of place mat, excluding fringe. Cut 2 lengths of trim the determined measurement. Glue lengths along top and bottom edges of place mat. Allow to dry flat.

MERRY MEMORY ALBUMS

COVERED PHOTO ALBUMS

This year, why not present Mom with a gift that's not only beautiful, but practical, too! Our holiday photo albums are perfect for storing precious memories of Christmases past. Covered in rich Yuletide fabrics, the albums are simple to craft using a little hot glue and dimensional paint. Tie them off with colorful ribbon or gold cord for festive closures.

You will need a photo album, low-loft polyester bonded batting, coordinating dimensional paint in squeeze bottles with very fine tips (we used green, red, and gold), lightweight cardboard, hot glue gun, and glue sticks.

For appliquéd album, you will **also** need fabric to cover album (we used red silk), fabric with motif for appliqué, paper-backed fusible web, and 1 yd of 1¹/₂"w ribbon.

For dimensional print album, you will **also** need print fabric to cover album and 2¹/₄ yds of ³/₈" dia. gold twisted cord.

APPLIQUÉD ALBUM

1. To cover outside of album, measure length (top to bottom) and width of open album. Cut a piece of batting the determined measurements. Cut a piece of fabric 2" larger on all sides than batting.

2. Glue batting to outside of album.

3. Center open album on wrong side of fabric piece. Fold corners of fabric diagonally over corners of album; glue in place. Fold short edges of fabric over side edges of album; glue in place. Fold long edges of fabric over top and bottom edges of album, trimming fabric to fit approx. ¹/₄" under binding hardware; glue in place.

4. To cover inside of album, cut two 2"w fabric strips 1" shorter than length (top to bottom) of album. Press ends of each strip ¹/₄" to wrong side. Center and glue 1 strip along each side of binding hardware with 1 long edge of each strip tucked approx. ¹/₄" under hardware.

5. Cut 2 pieces of cardboard ¹/₂" smaller on all sides than front of album. Cut 2 pieces of fabric 1" larger on all sides than 1 cardboard piece.

6. Center 1 cardboard piece on wrong side of 1 fabric piece. Fold corners of fabric diagonally over corners of cardboard piece; glue in place. Fold edges of fabric over edges of cardboard piece; glue in place. Repeat to cover remaining cardboard piece. Center and glue covered cardboard pieces inside front and back of album.

7. For appliqué, follow manufacturer's instructions to fuse web to wrong side of appliqué fabric; cut desired motif from fabric. Remove paper backing; fuse motif to album.

8. Use paint to paint over raw edges and details of appliqué. Allow to dry.

9. For ties, cut ribbon in half. Press end of 1 ribbon length ¹/₂" to wrong side. Center pressed end of ribbon length along right edge inside front of album; glue in place. Repeat to attach remaining ribbon length to right edge inside back of album. Trim ribbon ends.

DIMENSIONAL PRINT ALBUM

1. Follow Steps 1 - 6 of Appliquéd Album instructions to cover album, making sure fabric motif to be embellished is positioned as desired on front of album.

2. Use paint to paint over outlines and details of desired motif on cover. Allow to dry.

3. For ties, cut cord in half. Fold 1 length of cord in half. Referring to **Fig. 1**, knot cord near fold. Center knot along right edge of front cover of album; glue in place. Knot each end of cord; fray ends. Repeat to attach remaining length of cord to right edge on back of album.

Fig. 1

CANDYLAND FUNWEAR

Create holiday funwear when you stencil whimsical designs and add colorful trims to ready-made clothing. The simple shapes and colors on these fun pieces make the stencils a breeze to cut out and paint. Surprise a special little boy with this choo-choo train sweatshirt, loaded with a cargo of buttons. Or delight a teen with a sweet array of cookies and candies on a fleecy cardigan. Just stencil, add buttons, and glue on a bit of glitter, rickrack, and bows for a wearable holiday treat!

CHOO-CHOO SWEATSHIRT

You will need a child's sweatshirt; acetate for stencils; craft knife; cutting mat or thick layer of newspapers; removable tape (optional); paper towels; red, blue, and green fabric paint; stencil brushes; buttons; thread to sew on buttons; permanent felt-tip pen with fine point; and a T-shirt form or cardboard covered with waxed paper.

1. Wash, dry, and press sweatshirt according to paint manufacturer's recommendations. Insert T-shirt form into shirt.
2. Using train pattern, page 118, and green, blue, and red paint, follow **Stenciling**, page 123, to stencil train on shirt. For wheels, use red paint and peppermint pattern, page 118, to stencil peppermints on shirt.
3. Sew buttons to shirt above middle car on train.
4. To launder, follow paint manufacturer's recommendations.

COOKIES AND CANDY CARDIGAN

You will need a white V-neck jersey knit cardigan with pockets; acetate for stencils; permanent felt-tip pen with fine point; craft knife; cutting mat or thick layer of newspapers; removable tape (optional); paper towels; light brown and red fabric paint; stencil brushes; iridescent glitter; buttons to replace buttons on cardigan, assorted buttons for tops of cookies, and coordinating thread (optional); 3/8"w satin ribbon for bows; red and green rickrack; small safety pins; T-shirt form or cardboard covered with waxed paper; and washable fabric glue.

1. Wash, dry, and press cardigan according to paint manufacturer's recommendations. Insert T-shirt form into cardigan.
2. Using light brown paint and cookie patterns, page 118, follow **Stenciling**, page 123, to stencil cookies on cardigan. Using red paint and peppermint pattern, page 118, stencil peppermints on cardigan.
3. For "sugar" on each cookie, spread a thin layer of glue on cookie to 1/4" from edges. Before glue dries, sprinkle with glitter; allow to dry and gently shake off excess glitter.
4. If desired, sew buttons to centers of some cookies and replace buttons on cardigan.
5. For bow on each bell cookie, tie a 12" length of ribbon into a bow; trim ends. Using safety pin on wrong side of cardigan, pin bow to top of bell cookie.
6. For trim on neck and placket band, glue red rickrack along inner edge on 1 half of band from top of waistband to center back of neck band, trimming to fit. Repeat to glue green rickrack along remaining half of neck and placket band.
7. For trim on each pocket, glue a length of rickrack along top seam of pocket, trimming rickrack to fit.
8. To launder, remove bows and follow paint and glue manufacturers' recommendations.

COZY COASTERS

A country friend will adore a basket of these cute padded coasters! The simple Christmas tree shape is sewn from homespun fabric and soft batting and topped with a torn-fabric bow and a button. These festive coasters will be cozy keepers for hot holiday toddies.

CHRISTMAS TREE COASTERS

For each coaster, you will need two 7" squares of green print fabric, thread to match fabric, a 7" square of polyester bonded batting, a ⅝" x 5" torn fabric strip for bow, a ½" dia. button, pinking shears, and a removable fabric marking pen.

1. Use tree pattern, page 114, and follow **Tracing Patterns**, page 123.
2. Use fabric marking pen to draw around tree pattern on right side of 1 fabric square (back of coaster).
3. Place batting on wrong side of remaining fabric square; place back of coaster right side up on batting and pin layers together. Sew pieces together along drawn line. Leaving a ¼" seam allowance, use pinking shears to cut out coaster.
4. Form fabric strip into a bow shape and pinch together at center. Center bow at top of tree, place button on bow, and sew button and bow to tree at the same time.

NORTH WOODS THROW

Dressed up with fabric appliqués, this rustic throw will bring country warmth to a friend's home. The merry moose and other simple shapes are easy to cut out and fuse in place on a purchased wool afghan (or one you make with a length of wool fabric). Enhance the woodsy look with charming blanket stitching for a snuggly gift you'll finish in no time!

RUSTIC CHRISTMAS THROW

You will need a purchased approx. 43" x 63" wool afghan **or** a 43" x 63" piece of wool fabric with thread to match, fabrics for appliqués, coordinating embroidery floss for appliqués and wool yarn for edging on afghan, paper-backed fusible web, and tracing paper.

1. (**Note:** If purchased afghan is used, begin with Step 2.) To finish edges of wool fabric piece, use matching thread and a wide zigzag stitch with a short stitch length to stitch over raw edges of fabric piece.
2. Follow manufacturer's instructions to fuse web to wrong sides of appliqué fabrics. Do not remove paper backing.
3. For tree square appliqué, trace tree half pattern, page 120, onto tracing paper; cut out. Cut a 5" fabric square. Matching right sides, fold fabric square in half diagonally. Center dotted line of pattern on fold of

fabric square and draw around pattern. Carefully cutting through both layers of fabric, cut out tree. Discard tree shape.
4. For triangle appliqués, cut a 4" and a 3" fabric square; cut each square in half diagonally.
5. For moose appliqués, trace moose pattern, page 120, onto tracing paper; cut out. Use pattern to cut 2 moose from fabric (1 in reverse).

6. Remove paper backing from appliqués. Arrange tree square, triangles, and moose along 1 short edge of afghan; fuse in place.
7. Use 4 strands of embroidery floss to work **Blanket Stitch**, page 123, along raw edges of appliqués.
8. Use 2 strands of yarn to work **Blanket Stitch**, page 123, along same short edge of afghan.

TREATS IN A WINK

Whether you're preparing a unique gift from your kitchen or an impressive feast, our easy recipes will be ready in the wink of an eye! We've made them all super-quick by using packaged mixes, prepared foods, and basic ingredients. You'll find lots of irresistible treats with creative gift packaging, as well as no-fuss dishes for potlucks or serving unexpected guests. And our full menu of simplified dinner favorites will get you out of the kitchen in time to join all the merriment!

FOR YOUR "DEERS"

*F*or a sweet surprise, deliver individually wrapped pieces of Nutty Maple Fudge in a cute reindeer basket! The buttery candy is brimming with crunchy pecans for an unforgettable flavor combination. The festive container is surprisingly easy to make — simply glue toy reindeer pieces to a plain basket and then finish it with sprigs of holly and holiday ribbon. What an adorable way to share homemade goodies with those you hold "deer"!

NUTTY MAPLE FUDGE

- ¹/₄ cup butter or margarine
- ¹/₂ cup maple syrup
- 1 tablespoon milk
- 1 teaspoon vanilla extract
- 4¹/₂ cups sifted confectioners sugar
- 1 cup chopped pecans

Line an 8-inch square pan with aluminum foil, extending foil over 2 sides of pan; grease foil. In a heavy large saucepan, melt butter over medium-low heat. Add maple syrup, milk, and vanilla to butter, stirring until well blended. Remove from heat; add confectioners sugar, stirring until smooth. Stir in pecans. Spread mixture into prepared pan. Chill until firm. Use ends of foil to lift fudge from pan. Cut into 1-inch squares. Store in an airtight container.

Yield: about 50 pieces fudge

REINDEER BASKET

You will need a 3"h stuffed reindeer head and approx. 3" long stuffed reindeer legs (available at craft stores), a basket (our basket measures 5"w x 7"l x 4¹/₂"h), ³/₄"w and 1¹/₄"w ribbon, 2 silk holly sprigs with berries, hot glue gun, and glue sticks.

1. Measure around rim of basket; add ¹/₂". Cut a length of 1¹/₄"w ribbon the determined measurement. Glue ribbon around rim of basket, overlapping ends at back.

2. Glue reindeer head to back of basket at rim. Glue 1 reindeer front leg to each side of basket at rim. Glue reindeer hind legs to front of basket.

3. Tie a 12" length of ³/₄"w ribbon into a bow; trim ends. Glue bow to neck of reindeer head.

4. Tie a 25" length of 1¹/₄"w ribbon into a 4¹/₂"w bow; trim ends. Glue bow to front of basket; glue streamers of bow to reindeer front legs.

5. Glue 1 holly sprig to reindeer head and 1 to large bow.

CHRISTMAS PIE

*W*ith this special gift, "Happy Christmas" greetings go along with a scrumptious treat! Fast and easy to make, our Chocolate-Covered Cherry Pie is a tasty mixture of purchased candies and vanilla ice cream in a ready-made chocolate crust. Maraschino cherries and chocolate sprinkles top off the cool confection. Our decorative hand-punched pan, simple and quick to craft, brings country charm to your presentation.

CHOCOLATE-COVERED CHERRY PIE

1 quart vanilla ice cream, softened
1 box (8 ounces) chocolate-covered cherries, quartered
1 9-inch purchased chocolate crumb pie crust
8 maraschino cherries with stems (undrained) and chocolate sprinkles to garnish

In a medium bowl, combine ice cream and chocolate-covered cherries. Spoon ice cream mixture into crust. Dip maraschino cherries in chocolate sprinkles and place on pie to garnish. Add additional chocolate sprinkles to pie as desired. Place in freezer until firm.

Yield: about 8 servings

"HAPPY CHRISTMAS" PIE PAN

You will need a 9" aluminum pie pan, hammer, awl or large nail, muriatic acid (available at hardware stores), a 5-gallon plastic bucket, tongs, rubber gloves, paper towels, thick layer of newspapers, removable transparent tape, and tracing paper.

Note: Pie pan is for decorative use only. Line pan with aluminum foil or glass pan before using.

1. Trace pattern, page 121, onto tracing paper; cut out pattern along solid line.
2. Place pattern right side up in bottom of pan; tape in place. Place pan on newspapers. Use hammer and awl to lightly punch pan where indicated by dots on pattern, making indentations instead of holes. Remove pattern.
3. (**Note:** Muriatic acid is used to remove shiny surface from pan. Follow manufacturer's instructions and practice caution when using acid; wear rubber gloves and work in a well-ventilated area.) Pour acid into bucket to a depth of approx. 2". Fill remainder of bucket with water to approx. 2" from top. Using tongs, place pan into acid for several minutes; when surface of pan begins to bubble, remove from acid and rinse well with water. Place pan on paper towels and pat dry.

CORDIAL SNOWMAN

*L*et a cordial gift of
Raspberry Cream Liqueur
bring a smile to the face of
someone special. A blend
of only three ingredients,
the rich, fruity drink is extra-
easy to make. Present your
treat in a friendly snowman
bag and add frosty fun to
your surprise.

RASPBERRY CREAM LIQUEUR

2   cups whipping cream
2   cups half and half
1¼ cups framboise (raspberry brandy)

In a ½-gallon pitcher, combine all ingredients. Pour into a gift bottle with lid and store in refrigerator. Give with instructions to serve chilled.

Yield: about seven 6-ounce servings

SNOWMAN BOTTLE BAG

You will need muslin, thread to match muslin, a 2" x 16" torn fabric strip for scarf, two ½" dia. shank buttons for eyes, three ¾" dia. buttons for front of snowman, a ¼" x 3" stick for nose, orange acrylic paint, small paintbrush, a 3" dia. black felt top hat, a ½" x 7" strip of fabric for trim on hat, a 1"h artificial bird, red permanent felt-tip pen with fine point, instant coffee, craft knife, tissue paper, 2 rubber bands, hot glue gun, and glue sticks.

1. Measure around bottle; divide measurement by 2 and add 1½". Measure bottle from 1 side of lid to opposite side of lid (**Fig. 1**); add 7". Cut a piece of muslin the determined measurements.

Fig. 1

2. Dissolve 1 tablespoon instant coffee in 1 cup hot water; allow to cool. Soak muslin in coffee several minutes; remove from coffee, allow to dry, and press.

3. Matching short edges, fold muslin in half; finger press folded edge (bottom of bag). Using a ¼" seam allowance and thread to match muslin, sew sides of bag together.

4. Match each side seam to fold line at bottom of bag; sew across each corner 1" from point (**Fig. 2**). Turn bag right side out.

Fig. 2

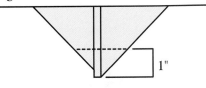

5. Place bottle in bag. For head, wrap 1 rubber band around bag approx. 3" from top of bottle. Stuff tissue paper into bag around top of bottle, forming a round shape. Wrap remaining rubber band around fabric bag just above top of bottle.

6. Tie torn fabric strip around snowman's neck for scarf.

7. For nose, use craft knife to shape 1 end of stick to a point; cut 1" of pointed end from stick. Paint pointed stick orange; allow to dry. Glue stick to head. Glue ½" dia. buttons to head for eyes. Use red pen to draw mouth.

8. Spacing buttons evenly, glue ¾" dia. buttons to front of snowman.

9. To decorate hat, glue remaining fabric strip around crown of hat. Glue bird to rim of hat. Place hat on head.

Bacon-Mushroom
Casserole

*O*ur easy and delicious
*Bacon-Mushroom Casserole
will help your neighbors rise
and shine! The delectable
meal combines four simple
ingredients with a creamy egg
mixture for a cheesy delight.
Prepare and deliver it to their
home on Christmas Eve, and
your neighbors will have a
yummy breakfast ready to
pop in the oven on Christmas
morning. Present the dish
with a quick-to-make "holly-
day" table runner and tag for
a cozy Yuletide finish.*

BACON-MUSHROOM CASSEROLE

Prepare and give casserole the day before it is to be served.

> 1 box (6 ounces) garlic and
>   onion croutons (about 3 cups)
> 1 can (4 ounces) sliced mushrooms,
>   drained
> 1 jar (2 ounces) real bacon pieces
> 1 package (8 ounces) shredded
>   Colby and Monterey Jack
>   cheeses
> 7 eggs
> 1 3/4 cups half and half

In a greased 9 x 13-inch baking dish, layer first 4 ingredients. In a medium bowl, whisk eggs and half and half; pour over cheeses. Cover and refrigerate until ready to present. Give with serving instructions.

Yield: about 12 servings

To serve: Store in refrigerator overnight. Bake uncovered casserole in a preheated 350-degree oven 30 to 35 minutes or until a knife inserted in center comes out clean. Allow casserole to stand 5 minutes before serving.

HOLLY TABLE RUNNER

You will need medium weight cotton or cotton blend fabric for runner, a 6" x 13" piece of green wool fabric for leaves, six 7/8" dia. red buttons, red embroidery floss, tracing paper, and paper-backed fusible web.

1. Cut a piece of fabric to desired finished size of table runner. Fringe edges of fabric piece 1/4".
2. For leaves, follow manufacturer's instructions to fuse web to wrong side of green fabric piece. Trace leaf pattern onto tracing paper; cut out. Use pattern to cut 4 leaves from fabric piece. Remove paper backing from leaves.
3. Fuse 2 leaves to each end of table runner, leaving approx. 1" of space between each pair of leaves. Use floss to work **Running Stitch**, page 123, approx. 1/8" inside edges of leaves and to sew 3 buttons between each pair of leaves for berries.

POPCORN GIFT TIN

*P*opcorn lovers will go nuts over this gift tin of Nutty Butterscotch Popcorn! Our gourmet snack, glazed with melted butterscotch chips and studded with crunchy peanuts, is a quick-and-easy gift to make ahead of time. Stored and presented in a painted Christmas tin, this gift will spread cheer by the handfuls.

NUTTY BUTTERSCOTCH POPCORN

- 1 package (12 ounces) butterscotch chips
- 16 cups unsalted popped popcorn
- 1 can (16 ounces) salted peanuts

Place butterscotch chips in a small microwave-safe bowl. Microwave on high power (100%) about 3 minutes, stirring every minute until chips are melted. Place popcorn and peanuts in a very large bowl. Pour melted chips over popcorn mixture; stir until well coated. Spread on greased aluminum foil; allow to cool. Store in an airtight container.

Yield: about 20 cups flavored popcorn

DECORATED POPCORN TIN

You will need a large popcorn tin with lid (ours measures 10¼" dia. x 8"h), spray primer, dark green and cream spray paint, dark green acrylic paint for holly leaves, a Miracle Sponge™ (dry, compressed sponge; available at craft stores), fabric for trim, red felt for holly berries, drawing compass, pinking shears, paper plate, paper towels, tracing paper, white vinegar, fabric marking pencil, hot glue gun, and glue sticks.

1. Wash tin and lid in hot soapy water (do not use lemon-scented soap); rinse well. Rinse can in a solution of 1 part vinegar and 1 part water. Dry completely.
2. Allowing to dry between coats, spray outside of tin and lid with several light coats of primer. Spray paint tin dark green and lid cream; allow to dry.
3. For berry pattern, use compass to draw a 1" dia. circle on tracing paper; trace leaf pattern onto tracing paper. Cut out patterns.
4. For leaves, use leaf pattern to cut leaf from sponge. Pour a small amount of dark green acrylic paint onto paper plate. Dip dampened sponge in paint and remove excess on a paper towel. Using a light stamping motion and reapplying paint to sponge as needed, sponge paint leaves in pairs along edge of lid; allow to dry.
5. For berries, use fabric marking pencil to draw around berry pattern on felt. Use pinking shears to cut berries from felt. Glue 1 berry to lid between each pair of leaves.
6. For trim, measure width of side of lid and add 1"; measure around lid and add 2". Cut a strip of fabric the determined measurements. Press all edges of fabric strip ½" to wrong side. Glue strip to side of lid, overlapping ends.

SAUCY POINSETTIAS

A friend who relishes holiday entertaining will adore a gift of zesty Jezebel Sauce. This tasty condiment offers an unusual blend of pineapple preserves, apple jelly, piquant horseradish, and mustard — and it's delicious with meats or appetizers. To dress up your gift, gather a pretty napkin around the jar and secure it at the top with our napkin ring that's easily crafted using a silk poinsettia. Include a set of matching napkins and rings to add a distinctive accent to an elegant table setting.

JEZEBEL SAUCE

- 1 jar (18 ounces) pineapple preserves
- 1 jar (18 ounces) apple jelly
- 1 jar (6 ounces) prepared horseradish
- 6 tablespoons prepared horseradish mustard

Combine all ingredients with an electric mixer or in a food processor; mix until well blended. Cover and store in refrigerator. Give with instructions to serve with meat or cream cheese and crackers.

Yield: about 4 cups sauce

NAPKIN RINGS AND JAR COVER

For each napkin ring, you will need a purchased brass napkin ring; 22" each of 1/16" dia. metallic gold cord, 1/8" dia. metallic red cord, and 3/8"w red satin ribbon; 3 3/4"w silk poinsettia with leaves; hot glue gun; and glue sticks.

For jar cover, you will need a cloth napkin with decorative edges (our napkin measures 17" square) and 1 napkin ring.

1. For napkin ring, tie lengths of cord and ribbon into a bow around napkin ring. Glue silk poinsettia with leaves to cord and ribbon beside bow.

2. For jar cover, place jar at center of napkin. Gather edges of napkin around top of jar. Thread gathered edges through napkin ring; arrange gathers.

ROLL OUT THE ELEGANCE

*T*hese Dried Fruit-Nut
Rolls are so deliciously rich,
no one will believe how easy
they are to prepare! Simply
chop the ingredients in a
food processor, shape the
mixture into logs, roll them
in shredded coconut, and
chill. To give the fruity logs
elegant flair, tuck them
in festive fabric wraps
and present them with a
coordinating decoupaged
serving plate.

DRIED FRUIT-NUT ROLLS

- 1 package (8 ounces) pitted dates
- 1 package (6 ounces) dried apricots
- 1³/₄ cups sweetened shredded coconut, divided
- 1 cup chopped pecans
- 2 tablespoons firmly packed brown sugar
- 2 tablespoons orange juice
- ¹/₂ teaspoon grated orange zest

Place dates, apricots, 1 cup coconut, pecans, brown sugar, orange juice, and orange zest in a food processor. Process until fruit and nuts are finely chopped. Shape mixture into two 6-inch-long rolls; roll in remaining ³/₄ cup coconut. Wrap in plastic wrap and store in refrigerator. Give with serving instructions to cut rolls into ¹/₄-inch slices.

Yield: 2 rolls, about 20 slices each

FRUIT ROLL WRAP

You will need a 7" x 12" fabric piece, a 6" square of lightweight cardboard, ¹/₂"w paper-backed fusible web tape, 1 yd each of ³/₈"w satin ribbon and ¹/₁₆" dia. gold twisted cord, and transparent tape.

1. Follow manufacturer's instructions to fuse web tape along short edges and 1 long edge on wrong side of fabric piece. Do not remove paper backing. Press fused edges to wrong side along inner edge of tape. Unfold edges and remove paper backing; refold edges and fuse in place.
2. Fuse a length of web tape to wrong side of fabric along long hemmed edge; remove paper backing. Overlap long hemmed edge ¹/₂" over remaining raw edge to form a tube; fuse edges together.
3. Roll cardboard into a tube, overlapping edges ¹/₂"; use transparent tape to tape overlapped edges together.
4. Cut ribbon and cord in half. Insert cardboard tube into fabric tube. Gather fabric at 1 end of tube; tie 1 length each of ribbon and cord together into a bow around fabric to secure. Place plastic-wrapped fruit roll inside tube. Gather fabric at remaining end of tube and tie with remaining ribbon and cord. Trim ends of ribbon and knot ends of cord.

DECOUPAGED PLATE

For each plate, you will need a clear glass plate, motif cut from fabric to fit on bottom of plate, ¹/₈"w gold braid trim, matte Mod Podge® sealer, acrylic paint to coordinate with motif, foam brushes, and clear varnish.

Note: Plate must be hand washed.

1. With right side of motif facing plate, use Mod Podge® sealer to glue motif to flat area on bottom of plate; glue gold braid trim along edge of flat area. Allow to dry.
2. Allowing to dry between coats, apply 2 coats of Mod Podge® sealer to bottom of plate.
3. Allowing to dry between coats, paint bottom of plate evenly with 2 coats of paint.
4. Being sure to cover edges of paint, apply 1 coat of varnish to bottom of plate; allow to dry.

GRANOLA GOODIE BOXES

When you need a bunch of easy last-minute gifts, mix up some Chocolate Granola Candies. One batch of this simple three-ingredient recipe makes several dozen bite-size candies that are given in foil cups for a candy-store look. For delivery, box them in painted Shaker boxes topped with giant fabric yo-yos and country accents.

CHOCOLATE GRANOLA CANDIES

2½ cups granola cereal with fruit and nuts
¾ cup diced mixed dried fruits and raisins
12 ounces chocolate-flavored candy coating

In a small bowl, combine cereal and dried fruits and raisins. In a heavy medium saucepan, melt candy coating over low heat; remove from heat. Stir cereal mixture into melted chocolate. Drop by teaspoonfuls into foil candy cups. Place candies in refrigerator to harden. Store in an airtight container in a cool, dry place.

Yield: about 5 dozen pieces candy

YO-YO SHAKER BOXES

For each box, you will need a round Shaker box (we used 4½", 5", and 7" dia. boxes), fabrics for yo-yo and trim, thread to match yo-yo fabric, acrylic paint to coordinate with fabrics, foam brush, fabric marking pencil, string, thumbtack, hot glue gun, and glue sticks.

For decoration on box, you will **also** need **either** a 1¼"w star-shaped wooden cutout, yellow acrylic paint, and a foam brush; a 2⅛"w heart-shaped wooden cutout and Design Master® glossy wood tone spray (available at craft stores and florist shops); **or** approx. 50" of jute twine and a ⅞" dia. button.

1. Remove lid from box and set aside. Allowing to dry between coats, paint outside of box.
2. For yo-yo, measure diameter of box lid; double measurement. Cut a square of fabric

the determined measurement. Fold fabric in half from top to bottom and again from left to right. Tie 1 end of string to fabric marking pencil. Measure diameter of lid again. Insert thumbtack through string the determined measurement from pencil. Insert thumbtack in fabric as shown in **Fig. 1** and mark ¼ of a circle. Cutting through all layers of fabric, cut out circle.

Fig. 1

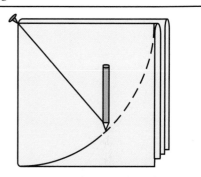

3. Use a double strand of thread to baste ⅛" from edge of fabric circle. Pull ends of thread to tightly gather circle; knot thread and trim ends. Flatten circle with gathers at center.
4. Glue yo-yo to top of box lid.
5. For trim, measure width of side of lid and add 1"; measure around lid and add 2". Cut a fabric strip the determined measurements. Press all edges ½" to wrong side. Glue strip to side of lid, overlapping ends.
6. For star decoration, paint star yellow and allow to dry; glue star to lid. For heart decoration, spray heart lightly with wood tone spray and allow to dry; glue heart to lid. For bow decoration, make a multi-loop bow from twine; glue bow to lid and glue button over bow.

"Beary" Jam

A "beary" sweet friend will adore this playful bag — especially when it holds a gift of Berry Christmas Jam. Delicious with breads, the easy preserves are an unusual combination of orange segments, cranberries, strawberries, and traditional holiday spices.

BERRY CHRISTMAS JAM

> 3 cups fresh cranberries
> 1 medium seedless orange, peeled and quartered
> 1 package (10 ounces) frozen sliced strawberries, slightly thawed
> 1/4 teaspoon ground cloves
> 1/4 teaspoon ground cinnamon
> 4 cups sugar
> 1/2 cup water
> 1 pouch (3 ounces) liquid fruit pectin

In a food processor, combine cranberries and orange quarters; process until coarsely chopped. Add strawberries, cloves, and cinnamon; process until mixture is finely chopped. In a heavy large saucepan, combine fruit mixture, sugar, and water until well blended. Stirring constantly over low heat, cook 2 minutes. Increase heat to high and bring mixture to a rolling boil. Stir in liquid pectin. Stirring constantly, bring to a rolling boil again and boil 1 minute. Remove from heat; skim off foam. Pour into heat-resistant jars with lids. Store in refrigerator.

Yield: about 3 pints jam

"BEARY" BAG

You will need a purchased white gift bag with handles; fabric for overalls and hat; a 1" x 18" fabric strip for bow on handle; pink, green, brown, and dark brown acrylic paint; small paintbrushes; a small sponge piece; black felt-tip pens with fine and medium points; white poster board for fabric insert and tag; craft knife; scrap cardboard; 6" of 1/8"w satin ribbon; white string; paper-backed fusible web; graphite transfer paper; tracing paper; hot glue gun; glue sticks; and a hole punch.

1. Trace bear pattern, page 122, onto tracing paper. Fold bag flat. Use transfer paper to transfer pattern to front of bag.

2. (**Note:** Allow to dry after each paint color.) Use damp sponge piece to lightly stamp brown paint onto bear's head, chest, arms, and feet. Use paintbrush and pink paint to paint cheeks. Use paintbrush and dark brown paint to paint inside of ear, muzzle, front paws, and tree trunk. Use paintbrush and green paint to paint remainder of tree.

3. Use black pen with medium point to draw over all transferred lines.

4. To cut out overalls and hat, cut a piece of scrap cardboard to fit inside bag; place cardboard inside bag next to bag front. Cutting inside pen lines, use craft knife to cut overalls and top portion of hat from bear design on bag. Remove cardboard.

5. For fabric insert, measure width of bag front; measure height of bag front and subtract 3/4". Cut 1 piece each of fabric and poster board the determined measurements. Follow manufacturer's instructions to fuse web to wrong side of fabric piece. Fuse fabric to poster board.

6. Open bag. Place fabric insert in bag. Use small dots of glue close to edges of cut out areas to glue insert to front of bag.

7. Tie ribbon into a bow; trim ends. Glue bow to point of hat.

8. Tie fabric strip into a bow around bag handle.

9. For tag, cut a 1 3/4" x 2 5/8" piece and a 1" x 2" piece of poster board. Center small poster board piece on large poster board piece and use black pen with fine point to draw around small piece. Do not remove small poster board piece. Holding small poster board piece firmly in place, use damp sponge piece to lightly stamp brown paint onto outer edge of large poster board piece; carefully remove small poster board piece and allow to dry.

10. Use black pen with fine point to write "You're Beary Sweet" on tag. Punch a hole in corner of tag and use string to tie tag to bow on bag handle.

*H*ere's a sweet gift for anyone on your holiday list! Chocolate-Dipped Peppermint Sticks are easy to make using melted chocolate. For a fun presentation, package the candy in clear cellophane bags tied with pretty ribbons. Then tuck the goodie bags in one of our festive cross stitch mini totes.

CHOCOLATE-DIPPED PEPPERMINT STICKS

3/4 cup semisweet chocolate chips
1 package (5½ ounces) red and white peppermint sticks (about eighteen 3-inch-long peppermint sticks)

In a small saucepan over low heat, melt chocolate chips. Dip one end of each peppermint stick into chocolate; place in small holes punched in a plastic foam block. Allow chocolate to harden. (**Note:** It's best to give candies on day of preparation. See **Using Chocolate**, page 124.)

Yield: about 18 peppermint sticks

CHRISTMAS MINI TOTES

For each tote, you will need an Ivory Aida (14 ct) Lil' Tote (5" x 5") and embroidery floss (see color key).

With design centered and top of design 1⅝" from top edge of tote, work design on tote, using 3 strands of floss for Cross Stitch, 2 for Backstitch for letters, 1 for all other Backstitch, and 2 for French Knots.

46w x 17h

39w x 17h

43w x 16h

CHRISTMAS MINI TOTES

X	DMC	1/4X	B'ST	ANC.	COLOR	X	DMC	1/4X	B'ST	ANC.	COLOR
★	blanc			2	white	◆	775			128	lt blue
◆	304			1006	dk red		898			360	dk brown
■	310			403	black	♥	909			923	dk green
✕	666			46	red	➕	912			209	green
━	761			1021	pink	●	666	French Knot		46	red

CRUNCHY MUNCHIES

A tin filled with zesty Curried Snack Sticks will be an irresistible treat for your favorite snacker. The crunchy mix of peanuts, pretzels, and potato sticks is coated with tangy spices for a fast and easy recipe. A "recycled" can painted with a wintry scene completes your peppery presentation.

CURRIED SNACK STICKS

- 1 can (16 ounces) salted peanuts
- 1 package (10 ounces) pretzel sticks
- 1 can (7 ounces) potato sticks
- 1/2 cup vegetable oil
- 2 packages (1.2 ounces each) curry sauce mix
- 1/2 teaspoon ground red pepper
- 1/2 teaspoon ground cumin seed

Preheat oven to 300 degrees. In a large bowl, combine peanuts, pretzel sticks, and potato sticks. In a small bowl, combine oil, curry sauce mix, red pepper, and cumin seed until well blended. Pour sauce mixture over peanut mixture; stir until well coated. Spread evenly in a large jellyroll pan. Bake 20 minutes, stirring after 10 minutes. Spread on aluminum foil to cool. Store in an airtight container.

Yield: about 14 cups snack mix

SNOW SCENE GIFT TIN

You will need a large can (we used a coffee can); white vinegar; grey spray primer; dark blue and white spray paint; white, green, and brown acrylic paint; flat paintbrushes; 1/4"w yellow star stickers; scrap paper; and tape.

1. Wash can in hot soapy water (do not use lemon-scented soap); rinse well. Rinse can in a solution of 1 part vinegar and 1 part water.

2. Allowing to dry between coats, spray can with several coats of primer.

3. (**Note:** Allow to dry after each paint color.) To make mask for hills on can, measure around can; cut a 2"w strip of paper the determined measurement. Tear away areas along 1 long edge of paper so paper strip resembles hills. With long straight edge of strip along bottom edge of can, tape strip around bottom of can. Spray paint can dark blue. Remove paper mask and allow to dry.

4. Using a flat paintbrush and white acrylic paint, use a stamping motion to paint over hills along bottom of can.

5. Spray can with a very light coat of white spray paint to resemble snow.

6. Using flat paintbrushes and a stamping motion, use green paint to paint triangular shapes for trees above hills and brown paint to paint tree trunks.

7. Use tip of a small paintbrush handle and white acrylic paint to paint dots on can for snowflakes.

8. Apply star stickers to can.

GINGERBREAD DELIGHT

A creamy topping makes our Gingerbread Bars a tasty variation of the traditional Christmas treat. They're deliciously fast and easy to make using a purchased cake mix! For a quick country touch, top the container with a gingerbread man cutout bordered with ribbon and buttons.

GINGERBREAD BARS

 1 package (14.5 ounces)
      gingerbread cake mix
 1/2 cup butter or margarine, melted
 3 eggs, divided
 1 package (8 ounces) cream cheese,
      softened
 4 1/2 cups sifted confectioners sugar

Preheat oven to 350 degrees. In a medium bowl, combine gingerbread mix, butter, and 1 egg. Spread mixture evenly into 2 greased 8-inch square baking pans. In a medium bowl, combine cream cheese, remaining 2 eggs, and confectioners sugar. Spread evenly over gingerbread layer in each pan. Bake 30 to 35 minutes or until lightly browned. Cool completely in pans. Cut into 1 x 2-inch bars. Store in an airtight container.

Yield: about 2 dozen bars in each pan

GINGERBREAD BOX

For each box, you will need an 8" square aluminum pan with clear plastic lid (we purchased ours from a grocery store), cream-colored paper, brown craft paper, red paper, 3/8"w plaid ribbon, four 7/8" dia. red buttons, black felt-tip pen with fine point, tracing paper, hot glue gun, and glue sticks.

1. Trace gingerbread man and heart patterns, page 122, onto tracing paper; cut out. Use patterns to cut gingerbread man from craft paper and heart from red paper.
2. Glue heart to center of gingerbread man.

3. Use black pen to draw eyes and mouth on gingerbread man and to draw dots and dashes along edge of gingerbread man to resemble stitching.
4. Cut a square from cream-colored paper to fit inside top of plastic lid. Glue gingerbread man to center of paper square. With gingerbread man facing lid, use glue only along edges of square to glue square inside top of lid.
5. Glue ribbon lengths along edges on top of lid. Glue 1 button to each corner over ribbon ends.

"GLOW WINE"

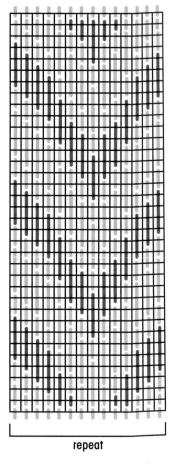

repeat

☑ red
☑ green
☑ metallic gold ribbon

A *dd a little Old World charm to a friend's holiday with a bottle of warming Glühwein, or "glow wine." A traditional German beverage, the fruity red wine is steeped with spices, including cinnamon, cloves, and nutmeg, and sweetened with brown sugar. Served hot, it's perfect for a Christmas toast! Include a festive bargello needlework mug for serving, and your gift will say "Guten Tag!"*

BARGELLO MUG

You will need red and green worsted weight yarn and Kreinik Balger® gold (#002) ⅛"w ribbon, 10 mesh plastic canvas, #20 tapestry needle, and a Crafter's Pride® Stitch-A-Mug™.

1. Follow thread count to cut plastic canvas piece. Follow chart and use Gobelin Stitches to work mug insert, repeating pattern until mug insert is completed. Use green Overcast Stitches to cover long unworked edges. Use green to join short edges, forming a cylinder.
2. Place insert in mug, aligning seam with handle. Remove stitched piece before washing mug.

GOBELIN STITCH

This basic stitch is worked over 2 or more threads or intersections. The number of threads or intersections may vary according to the chart (**Fig. 1**).

Fig. 1

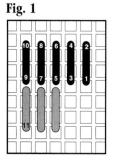

OVERCAST STITCH

This stitch covers the edge of the canvas (**Fig. 2**). It may be necessary to go through the same hole more than once to get even coverage on the edge, especially at the corners.

Fig. 2

GLÜHWEIN

  2 teaspoons ground cinnamon
  1 teaspoon dried lemon peel
¼ teaspoon ground cloves
¼ teaspoon ground allspice
¼ teaspoon ground nutmeg
  1 bottle (1.5 liters) burgundy wine
  2 cups firmly packed brown sugar

  Place spices in a 6-inch square of cheesecloth or a coffee filter; tie with a string. Combine wine and sugar in a Dutch oven. Add bundle of spices. Stirring constantly, cook over medium heat until sugar dissolves and wine is heated through. Remove spice bundle. Store in an airtight container in refrigerator. Give with instructions to serve drink hot.

Yield: about eight 6-ounce servings

*P*ainted in holiday hues and adorned with homespun trims, these converted food cans are the perfect size for presenting holiday treats like jars of tangy jelly or clusters of minty-sweet lollipops. Our Cranberry-Orange Jelly — tasty with toast or English muffins — is quick and easy to make using purchased fruit juices. Wrapped in plastic, the Christmas Candy Lollipops are tied with shiny bows for a festive presentation.

CRANBERRY-ORANGE JELLY

6½ cups sugar
4 cups cranberry juice cocktail
1 can (6 ounces) frozen orange juice concentrate, thawed
1 pouch (3 ounces) liquid fruit pectin

In a large Dutch oven, combine sugar and juices; stir until well blended. Stirring constantly over high heat, bring mixture to a rolling boil. Stir in liquid pectin. Stirring constantly, bring mixture to a rolling boil again and boil 1 minute. Remove from heat; skim off foam. Pour into heat-resistant jars with lids. Store in refrigerator.

Yield: about 4½ pints jelly

CHRISTMAS CANDY LOLLIPOPS

Vegetable cooking spray
2 medium-size red-white-and-green-striped candy canes
6 lollipop sticks
1 pound hard cinnamon candies (1-inch diameter)

Spray 3-inch-diameter indentations of a plastic 6-lollipop mold with cooking spray. Crush candy canes into coarse pieces. Place candy cane pieces and a lollipop stick in each indentation of mold. For each lollipop, place 10 to 12 cinnamon candies in a microwave-safe measuring cup. Microwave on high power (100%) 2 minutes, stirring after 1 minute. Pour melted candies over crushed candies in 1 indentation. Repeat for remaining lollipops. Allow to harden. Press on back of lollipop mold to release lollipops.

Yield: 6 lollipops

BUTTON-TRIMMED GIFT TINS

For each tin, you will need a can (we used roasted peanut and large vegetable cans), white vinegar, spray primer, hot glue gun, and glue sticks.

For button card tin, you will **also** need green spray paint, a 2¼" x 3" piece of heavy red paper, a 1½" x 2½" piece of heavy white paper, a black felt-tip pen with fine point, buttons, and embroidery floss (optional).

For button bow tin, you will **also** need red spray paint, fabric for bow, a button, and embroidery floss (optional).

BUTTON CARD TIN

1. Wash can in hot soapy water (do not use lemon-scented soap); rinse well. Rinse can in a solution of 1 part vinegar and 1 part water.

2. Allowing to dry between coats, spray can with several coats of primer.

3. Spray paint can green. Allow to dry.

4. For tag, glue white paper piece to red paper piece. Use black pen to draw dashed lines along edge of white paper piece to resemble stitching and to write "Merry Christmas!" on tag. If desired, thread floss through buttons to resemble stitching; knot floss at back. Glue buttons to tag. Glue tag to can.

BUTTON BOW TIN

1. Follow Steps 1 and 2 of Button Card Tin instructions.

2. Spray paint can red. Allow to dry.

3. Measure around can; add 7". Tear a 2"w strip of fabric the determined measurement.

4. Knot fabric strip around can. Place ends of strip over knot; using fingers, gather ends of strip to resemble a bow and glue in place.

5. If desired, thread floss through button to resemble stitching. Glue button to bow.

CHRISTMAS SNACK SACKS

*W*ith Santa and his trusty reindeer pal by your side, Christmas gift-giving is in the bag! Sweet morsels like our Rocky Road Candy and Fruitcake Cookies are perfect fillers for the holiday holders. The nutty fudge candy takes only a few minutes to make in the microwave, and the tasty cookies are made by blending leftover fruitcake with purchased sugar cookie mix. What a delicious idea!

ROCKY ROAD CANDY

1 cup semisweet chocolate chips
1 cup milk chocolate chips
1 jar (7 ounces) marshmallow
   creme
$2/3$ cup sweetened condensed milk
$1/2$ teaspoon vanilla extract
4 cups miniature marshmallows
2 cups chopped pecans, toasted

Line a 9 x 13-inch baking pan with aluminum foil, extending foil over ends of pan; grease foil. In a 3-quart microwave-safe bowl, combine chocolate chips. Microwave on medium-high power (80%) 3 minutes, stirring after $1^1/2$ minutes. Stir in marshmallow creme; microwave on medium-high power (80%) 1 minute. Add sweetened condensed milk and vanilla; stir until well blended. Add marshmallows and pecans; stir until well coated. Spread mixture into pan. Chill until firm. Use ends of foil to lift candy from pan. Cut into 1-inch squares. Store in an airtight container.

Yield: about 8 dozen pieces candy

FRUITCAKE COOKIES

1 package (15 ounces) sugar
   cookie mix and ingredients
   required to prepare cookies
$1^3/4$ cups chopped fruitcake

Preheat oven to 375 degrees. In a medium bowl, mix cookie dough according to package directions. Stir in fruitcake pieces. Drop rounded teaspoonfuls of dough 2 inches apart onto an ungreased baking sheet. Bake 6 to 8 minutes or until edges are lightly browned. Transfer cookies to a wire rack to cool completely. Store in an airtight container.

Yield: about 4 dozen cookies

REINDEER GIFT BAG

You will need a brown lunch-size paper bag, shiny red wrapping paper, black felt-tip pen with fine point, white and pink colored pencils, brown pipe cleaners, a $1^1/2$" x $1^3/4$" piece of tan burlap, spray adhesive, drawing compass, hot glue gun, and glue sticks.

1. For nose, use compass to draw a 2" dia. circle on wrong side of wrapping paper; cut out. Use spray adhesive to glue circle 6" below top of bag.
2. For face, use pen to draw eyes, eyebrows, and mouth on bag. Use white pencil to color eyes. Use pink pencil to color cheeks.
3. Place gift in bag.
4. Fold top of bag 1" to back; fold 1" to back again. Fold top corners of bag diagonally to back.
5. For antlers, cut two $7^1/2$" and two $4^1/2$" lengths from pipe cleaners. Place 1 end of 1 long pipe cleaner in fold of each corner at top of bag; glue in place. Twist 1 short pipe

cleaner length around each long pipe cleaner length; bend pipe cleaners to resemble antlers.
6. For hair, fringe burlap piece and glue to center top of bag.

SANTA GIFT BAG

You will need a white lunch-size paper bag, fabric for hat, $1^1/2$"w ribbon for hat trim, heavy white paper for mustache, a $7/8$" dia. red button for nose, a $1^3/4$" white pom-pom, black felt-tip pen with fine point, pink colored pencil, tracing paper, paper-backed fusible web, hot glue gun, and glue sticks.

1. For hat, follow manufacturer's instructions to fuse web to wrong side of fabric. Measure width and height of front of bag. Cut fabric piece same width and half the height of bag. Fuse fabric piece to top of bag.
2. For hat trim, measure width of bag; cut a length of ribbon the determined measurement. Cut a piece of web slightly smaller than ribbon. Fuse web to ribbon. Overlapping ribbon $1/4$" over bottom edge of hat fabric, fuse ribbon to bag.
3. For mustache, trace pattern onto tracing paper; cut out. Use pattern to cut mustache from heavy paper. Glue mustache to bag 1" below ribbon.
4. For face, use pen to draw eyes, eyebrows, and mouth on bag; use pink pencil to color cheeks and mouth. For nose, glue button to center of mustache.
5. Place gift in bag.
6. Fold top corners of bag diagonally to back to form point of hat. (If necessary, trim top edges of bag to allow bag to fold easily). Glue pom-pom to point of hat.

DELIGHTFUL QUICK DISHES

When it's time for Yuletide feasting, don't let the hectic holiday pace keep you from joining the fun! Made with purchased mixes and basic ingredients from the cupboard, the fast-and-easy recipes in this collection will fit right into your busy schedule. Each dish is incredibly simple — but so delicious that no one will believe you didn't spend hours in the kitchen. Any of them would be perfect for serving to drop-in guests, and some are even designed to travel well, so you can take them anywhere you're celebrating with friends. You can get the party started with spirited Cranberry Freezer Daiquiris. Or you may want to tempt hearty appetites with our tasty Southwest Olive Bread or tangy Sweet-and-Sour Pork Chops. These delicious dishes will ensure a happy holiday season!

CRANBERRY FREEZER DAIQUIRIS

- 2 to 3 cups crushed ice
- 1 can (16 ounces) jellied cranberry sauce
- 1 can (10 ounces) frozen strawberry daiquiri mix
- 1¼ cups rum
- 2 tablespoons grenadine syrup

  Fresh or frozen whole strawberries to garnish

In a blender or food processor, combine crushed ice, cranberry sauce, daiquiri mix, rum, and grenadine syrup; blend until slushy. Store in an airtight container in freezer. To serve, garnish with strawberries.

Yield: about seven 6-ounce servings

SWEET-AND-SOUR PORK CHOPS

- 8 boneless pork chops (about 1½ pounds)
- 2 tablespoons vegetable oil
- 1 can (16 ounces) shredded sauerkraut, drained
- 1 can (20 ounces) apple pie filling
- 1 medium green pepper, sliced into rings
- 1 medium sweet red pepper, sliced into rings

Preheat oven to 350 degrees. In an ovenproof skillet, lightly brown pork chops in oil over medium-high heat. Layer sauerkraut and pie filling over pork chops. Place pepper rings over pie filling. Cover and bake 55 to 60 minutes or until pork is tender. Serve warm.

Yield: 8 servings

Our Stuffed Gouda Cheese, a speedy South-of-the-Border appetizer, is perfect for serving at home or at a potluck. Prepared ahead of time, it's delicious warmed in the microwave and presented with flour tortillas.

SOUTHWEST OLIVE BREAD

- 3 cups self-rising yellow cornmeal mix
- 1 teaspoon ground cumin
- ¼ teaspoon ground red pepper
- 1½ cups milk
- 2 eggs
- ¼ cup vegetable oil
- 1 cup (4 ounces) shredded sharp Cheddar cheese
- 2 jars (5¾ ounces each) whole stuffed green olives, drained

Preheat oven to 375 degrees. In a medium bowl, combine cornmeal mix, cumin, and red pepper. Add milk, eggs, and oil; stir until well blended. Add remaining ingredients, stirring well. Spoon batter into 4 greased and floured 3 x 5½-inch loaf pans. Bake 35 to 40 minutes or until bread is golden brown and a toothpick inserted in center of bread comes out clean. Cool in pans on a wire rack 5 minutes. Run a knife around edges of pans to loosen bread; remove from pans. Serve warm.

Yield: 4 mini loaves bread

STUFFED GOUDA CHEESE

- 1 round (about 7 ounces) Gouda cheese, rind removed
- 1 can (3½ ounces) bean dip
- 2 tablespoons salsa
- 1 package (10 ounces) 7-inch flour tortillas, divided

  Pickled jalapeño pepper slices to garnish

Hollow out cheese round, leaving about a 1-inch shell of cheese; reserve pieces of cheese. In a small bowl, combine bean dip and salsa. Spoon bean mixture into cheese shell. Place 1 flour tortilla in a microwave-safe dish. Place reserved cheese pieces and filled cheese round on top of tortilla; cover loosely with plastic wrap. Microwave on medium-high power (80%) 1 to 2 minutes or until cheese is soft enough to spread. Garnish with jalapeño pepper slices. Serve warm with remaining flour tortillas.

Yield: 1 stuffed cheese round

CHEESY CRAB TOASTS

Cheese mixture can be made 1 day in advance and chilled.

    2 small (2¼ x 14 inches each) French
          bread loaves (1 pound total)
    2 cups (8 ounces) shredded sharp
          Cheddar cheese
    1 can (6 ounces) crabmeat, drained
  ⅓ cup mayonnaise
    2 teaspoons prepared horseradish
    1 teaspoon dried chopped chives

Preheat oven to 375 degrees. Cut each French bread loaf in half lengthwise. Combine cheese, crabmeat, mayonnaise, horseradish, and chives in a food processor until smooth. Spread cheese mixture over each loaf half. Bake on an ungreased baking sheet 20 to 25 minutes or until cheese mixture is hot and edges of bread are lightly browned. Cut into 1-inch slices. Serve warm.

Yield: about 52 appetizers

ZESTY RIPE OLIVE DIP

    1 can (10 ounces) diced tomatoes
          and green chilies, well drained
    2 cans (4½ ounces each) chopped
          green chilies, well drained
    2 cans (4¼ ounces each) chopped
          ripe olives, well drained
    1 tablespoon red wine vinegar
    2 teaspoons olive oil
  ½ teaspoon ground black pepper

For a colorful treat, stir up our Zesty Ripe Olive Dip and allow its spicy flavors to blend until party time. Delicious appetizers for an at-home gathering, Cheesy Crab Toasts feature piquant horseradish and sharp Cheddar cheese.

  ¼ teaspoon salt
  ¼ teaspoon garlic powder
       Tortilla chips to serve

In a medium bowl, combine tomatoes and green chilies, chopped green chilies, ripe olives, vinegar, oil, pepper, salt, and garlic powder. Cover and allow mixture to stand 1 hour for flavors to blend. Serve at room temperature with tortilla chips.

Yield: about 2⅔ cups dip

CHEESE DANISH PASTRIES

- 4 ounces (1/2 of an 8-ounce package) cream cheese, softened
- 1/4 cup sifted confectioners sugar
- 1 egg yolk
- 1/2 teaspoon lemon extract
- 1 can (8 ounces) refrigerated crescent rolls

Preheat oven to 375 degrees. In a small bowl, beat cream cheese, confectioners sugar, egg yolk, and lemon extract with an electric mixer until well blended. Unroll crescent roll dough on a lightly greased surface; firmly press dough perforations together to form a 7 1/2 x 14 1/2-inch rectangle. Spread cream cheese mixture over dough to within 1/2 inch of edges. Beginning at 1 long edge, roll up dough jellyroll-style. Using a serrated knife, cut into 3/4-inch slices. Place slices 2 inches apart on a lightly greased baking sheet. Bake 11 to 13 minutes or until lightly browned. Serve warm.

Yield: about 16 pastries

CHOCOLATE CINNAMON ROLLS

- 1 can (8 ounces) refrigerated crescent rolls
- 2 tablespoons butter or margarine, softened
- 1/2 cup semisweet chocolate mini chips
- 2 tablespoons sugar
- 2 tablespoons chopped pecans
- 1 1/2 teaspoons ground cinnamon

Preheat oven to 375 degrees. Unroll crescent roll dough on a lightly greased surface; firmly press dough perforations together to form a 7 1/2 x 14 1/2-inch rectangle. Spread butter over dough. In a small bowl, combine chocolate chips, sugar, pecans, and cinnamon. Sprinkle

They're so rich and yummy, who could guess that both of these pastries are made from canned crescent rolls! Overnight guests will happily awaken to the aroma of our buttery Chocolate Cinnamon Rolls. A sweetened cream cheese filling lends lemony flavor to Cheese Danish Pastries.

chocolate chip mixture over buttered dough to within 1/2 inch of edges. Lightly press mixture into dough. Beginning at 1 long edge, roll up dough jellyroll-style. Cut into 3/4-inch slices. Place slices 1 inch apart in a greased 9 x 13-inch baking pan. Bake 11 to 13 minutes or until lightly browned. Serve warm.

Yield: about 16 rolls

NUTTY FUDGE PIE

- 1 cup sugar
- ½ cup butter or margarine, melted
- ½ cup all-purpose flour
- ½ cup chopped pecans
- 2 eggs
- 3 tablespoons cocoa
- 1 teaspoon vanilla extract

  Ice cream and chopped pecans to serve

In a medium bowl, combine sugar, butter, flour, pecans, eggs, cocoa, and vanilla until well blended. Pour batter into a greased 9-inch microwave-safe pie plate. Microwave on medium power (60%) 10 to 12 minutes or until almost set in center (do not overbake). Serve warm with ice cream and pecans.

Yield: about 8 servings

SPICED COFFEE MIX

- 1 cup instant coffee granules
- ⅔ cup firmly packed brown sugar
- 2 teaspoons ground cinnamon

  Cinnamon sticks to garnish

Combine coffee granules, brown sugar, and cinnamon in a food processor; process until well blended. Store in an airtight container. To serve, stir 1 teaspoon coffee mix into 6 ounces hot water. Garnish with a cinnamon stick.

Yield: about 1½ cups coffee mix

When you need a luscious dessert for unexpected guests, try our microwavable Nutty Fudge Pie and you'll have a sweet treat in minutes. A warming mug of Spiced Coffee is just seconds away with a store of simple dry ingredients!

You'll have homemade flavor without all the work with this Brownie Nut Bread, which travels well for office potlucks and other holiday gatherings. To bring out the flavor of the bread, serve it with a generous amount of Creamy Cinnamon Spread — the perfect complement to the nutty, chocolaty loaves.

BROWNIE NUT BREAD

1 package (21.5 ounces) brownie mix
1 package (5.5 ounces) buttermilk biscuit mix
²/₃ cup water
2 eggs
¹/₄ cup vegetable oil
1 teaspoon vanilla extract
1 package (6 ounces) semisweet chocolate chips
1 cup chopped pecans
¹/₂ cup raisins

Preheat oven to 350 degrees. In a medium bowl, beat brownie mix, buttermilk biscuit mix, water, eggs, oil, and vanilla with an electric mixer until well blended. Stir in chocolate chips, pecans, and raisins until well blended. Pour batter into 2 lightly greased nonstick 4¹/₂ x 8¹/₂-inch loaf pans. Bake 45 to 50 minutes or until a toothpick inserted near center comes out with a few crumbs clinging to it. Cool in pans on a wire rack 10 minutes. Run a knife around edges of pans to loosen bread; remove from pans. Cool on wire rack 10 minutes longer. Serve warm with Creamy Cinnamon Spread.

Yield: 2 loaves bread

CREAMY CINNAMON SPREAD

1 package (8 ounces) cream cheese, softened
3 tablespoons sifted confectioners sugar
1 teaspoon ground cinnamon
¹/₂ teaspoon vanilla extract

In a small bowl, beat cream cheese, confectioners sugar, cinnamon, and vanilla with an electric mixer until well blended. Store in an airtight container in refrigerator. Serve at room temperature with Brownie Nut Bread.

Yield: about 1 cup spread

HOLIDAY ICE CREAM

¹/₂ gallon vanilla ice cream, softened
1 cup coarsely chopped red and green
    candied cherries
1 cup coarsely chopped walnuts
    Vegetable cooking spray

In a medium bowl, combine ice cream,
cherries, and walnuts. Spray 3¹/₂-inch-wide
by 4¹/₂-inch-high Christmas tree-shaped
molds with cooking spray. Spoon ice cream
mixture into molds; freeze until firm. To
unmold, hold bottoms of molds in warm
water a few seconds. Freeze in a single layer
in an airtight container until ready to serve.

Yield: about 20 ice-cream trees

CHAMPAGNE PUNCH

1 bottle (750 ml) champagne,
    chilled
1 bottle (10 ounces) club soda, chilled
³/₄ cup kirsch (cherry liqueur)

In a large serving container, combine
champagne, club soda, and kirsch. Serve
immediately.

Yield: about ten 4-ounce servings

*Festive candied cherries and
walnuts add Christmas cheer to
Holiday Ice Cream, especially when
formed in tree-shaped molds! Keep
them in the freezer and you'll be
prepared for an impromptu get-
together. Easy to pour up in a flash,
our bubbly Champagne Punch is
perfect for a Yuletide toast.*

FAST AND FESTIVE FARE

When friends and family gather to share a Yuletide feast, the spirit of the season fills the house. With all the cooking and baking, many people spend most of the day in the kitchen instead of with loved ones. But with our deliciously quick dishes, you'll have a full menu of traditional favorites in a fraction of the time! Our recipes start with purchased mixes and prepared items — but the results are so tempting, your guests will never guess how fast and simple they are. Shape up your meal with our yummy Turkey and Dressing Ring made with sliced turkey breast from the deli. Baked in a tree-shaped pan, Herbed Christmas Rolls begin with frozen yeast rolls. Apple pie filling and orange marmalade give our super-quick Fruited Sweet Potato Casserole a unique flavor. With this fabulously fast and festive fare, you'll spend less time in the kitchen and more time celebrating with your guests!

Topped with buttery cracker crumbs, our cheesy Green Beans au Gratin will be an instant favorite! The creamy side dish is stirred up quickly with simple ingredients and popped in the oven for an easy, tasty treat.

TURKEY AND DRESSING RING

1 pound ground turkey sausage
2 packages (8 ounces each) herb-seasoned stuffing mix
1 can (11 ounces) Mexican-style corn, drained
1 can (10³/4 ounces) cream of celery soup, undiluted
¹/2 cup frozen chopped onion
¹/2 cup frozen chopped green pepper
¹/2 cup chopped pecans
2 eggs
1 pound thinly sliced deli-style turkey breast
1 can (16 ounces) whole berry cranberry sauce

Preheat oven to 350 degrees. In a large bowl, combine sausage, stuffing mix, corn, soup, onion, green pepper, pecans, and eggs. Mix until ingredients are well blended. Press half of dressing into a greased 10-inch fluted tube pan. Layer turkey slices over dressing; lightly press remaining dressing into pan. Bake 60 to 65 minutes or until golden brown. Immediately invert onto a serving plate. Spoon cranberry sauce over hot dressing. Serve warm.

Yield: 12 to 14 servings

GREEN BEANS AU GRATIN

4 tablespoons butter or margarine, melted and divided
2 tablespoons all-purpose flour
1 cup sour cream
1 teaspoon minced dried onion
1 teaspoon sugar
¹/2 teaspoon salt
¹/4 teaspoon ground black pepper
¹/8 teaspoon ground red pepper
3 cans (16 ounces each) French-style green beans, drained
1 cup freshly shredded Parmesan cheese
1¹/2 cups butter-flavored cracker crumbs
2 teaspoons sesame seed

Preheat oven to 350 degrees. In a medium bowl, combine 2 tablespoons melted butter and flour. Add sour cream, onion, sugar, salt, black pepper, and red pepper; stir until well blended. Stir in green beans. Pour mixture into a greased 7 x 11-inch baking dish. Sprinkle cheese on top. In a small bowl, combine cracker crumbs, remaining 2 tablespoons melted butter, and sesame seed; sprinkle over cheese. Bake 35 to 40 minutes or until heated through and cracker crumbs are golden brown. Serve warm.

Yield: about 8 servings

HERBED CHRISTMAS ROLLS

1 package (25 ounces) frozen yeast rolls
1 large green pepper
1 large sweet red pepper
3 tablespoons butter or margarine
1 teaspoon dried dill weed

Place frozen rolls in a lightly greased 11-inch-wide x 15-inch-high Christmas tree-shaped cake pan. Cover and let rise according to package directions. Use a star-shaped aspic cutter to cut stars from peppers; cover with plastic wrap. Preheat oven to 375 degrees. Bake rolls 12 to 14 minutes or until golden brown; remove from pan.

In a small microwave-safe bowl, melt butter. Stir in dill weed. Brush butter mixture onto tops of rolls. Place pepper stars on tops of rolls. Serve warm.

Yield: 2 dozen rolls

FRUITED SWEET POTATO CASSEROLE

2 cans (17 ounces each) whole sweet potatoes, drained
1 cup bite-size pitted prunes
1 can (21 ounces) apple pie filling
1/2 cup orange marmalade
1 tablespoon firmly packed brown sugar
1/2 teaspoon ground cinnamon

Preheat oven to 350 degrees. Place sweet potatoes and prunes in a greased 8 x 11½-inch baking dish. Spoon apple pie filling over sweet potato mixture. In a small saucepan, melt marmalade over medium heat. Stir in brown sugar and cinnamon. Spoon marmalade mixture over fruit. Bake 30 to 35 minutes or until bubbly and heated through. Serve warm.

Yield: 8 to 10 servings

CRANBERRY-ORANGE GELATIN SALAD

1 unpeeled medium seedless orange, quartered
1 unpeeled medium red apple, quartered and cored
1 stalk celery, cut into 2-inch pieces
2 cups fresh cranberries
1 can (8¼ ounces) crushed pineapple packed in juice, undrained
3/4 cup chopped pecans
1 package (3 ounces) orange-flavored gelatin

Chopping the fruit, celery, and pecans in a food processor makes it easy to pack cool flavor into our Cranberry-Orange Gelatin Salad. The fruity salad is a light complement to a hearty meal. For a Yuletide touch, use cream cheese, parsley, and an orange-peel star to create a festive tree on top.

1 package (3 ounces) cherry-flavored gelatin
2 cups boiling water
Cream cheese, chopped parsley, and orange peel to garnish

In a food processor, combine orange, apple, and celery; process until coarsely chopped. Add cranberries, undrained pineapple, and pecans to food processor; process until mixture is finely chopped. In a large bowl, combine gelatins with boiling water; stir until gelatins are dissolved. Add cranberry mixture. Pour into a 6-cup gelatin mold; chill. To serve, unmold gelatin onto a serving plate. Garnish with cream cheese, chopped parsley, and orange peel. Serve chilled.

Yield: 10 to 12 servings

Our Apricot-Nut Fruitcake, made with packaged cake and pudding mixes, will give you a head start on your big event. Preparing it a day in advance allows its spirited glaze to reach peak flavor. Fudge-Topped Pumpkin Pie begins with a purchased frozen pie that you improve with a homemade glaze of melted chocolate chips, honey, orange extract, and pecans. Served warm, it's simply delicious!

FUDGE-TOPPED PUMPKIN PIE

1 9-inch frozen pumpkin pie (about 40 ounces)
1¼ cups semisweet chocolate chips
2 tablespoons honey
2 teaspoons vegetable shortening
¼ teaspoon orange extract
1 cup chopped pecans, toasted
Pecan halves to garnish

Bake pumpkin pie according to package directions. Remove from oven and place on a wire rack. Place chocolate chips in a small microwave-safe bowl. Microwave on medium-high power (80%) 1 minute; stir. Continue to microwave 15 seconds at a time, stirring until smooth. Add honey, shortening, and orange extract; stir until well blended. Stir in pecans. Spread topping over hot pie. Allow pie to cool 1 hour. Garnish with pecan halves and serve warm.

Yield: about 10 servings

APRICOT-NUT FRUITCAKE

Make at least 1 day in advance.

CAKE

1 package (18.25 ounces) yellow cake mix
1 package (8 ounces) cream cheese, softened
1 package (3.5 ounces) vanilla pudding and pie filling mix
4 eggs
⅓ cup vegetable oil
¼ cup water
¼ cup apricot brandy
1 package (6 ounces) dried apricots, coarsely chopped
2 cups coarsely chopped pecans

GLAZE

¼ cup apricot preserves
¼ cup apricot brandy

A steaming mug of Raspberry Cider will be the crowning touch for your delicious fare. It's simple to heat up in just minutes by combining apple cider, raspberry jelly, and soft drink mixes.

Preheat oven to 350 degrees. For cake, combine cake mix, cream cheese, pudding mix, eggs, oil, water, and brandy in a large bowl. Blend at low speed of an electric mixer until moistened. Beat at medium speed 2 minutes longer. Stir in apricots and pecans. Pour into a greased and floured 10-inch fluted tube pan. Bake 55 to 60 minutes or until a toothpick inserted in center of cake comes out clean. Allow cake to cool in pan 10 minutes. Invert onto a serving plate.

For glaze, combine preserves and brandy in a small bowl; spoon over warm cake. Cool cake completely. Cover and allow to stand at room temperature 24 hours before serving.

Yield: about 16 servings

RASPBERRY CIDER

1 quart apple cider
1 jar (12 ounces) raspberry jelly
1 teaspoon presweetened lemonade-flavored soft drink mix
⅛ teaspoon unsweetened raspberry-flavored soft drink mix
Fresh lemon slices to serve

In a large saucepan, bring cider to a simmer. Add jelly and drink mixes, stirring until jelly is dissolved. Serve hot with lemon slices.

Yield: about seven 6-ounce servings

PATTERNS

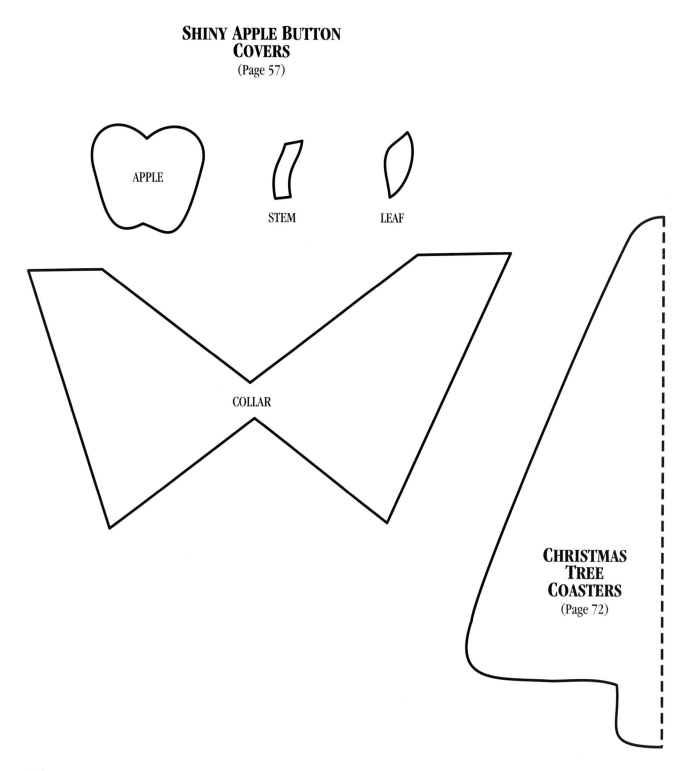

SHINY APPLE BUTTON
COVERS
(Page 57)

APPLE

STEM

LEAF

COLLAR

CHRISTMAS
TREE
COASTERS
(Page 72)

CHRISTMAS CARDS
AND ENVELOPES
(Page 42)

PRETTY POINSETTIA
APRON
(Page 53)

POT

PATTERNS (continued)

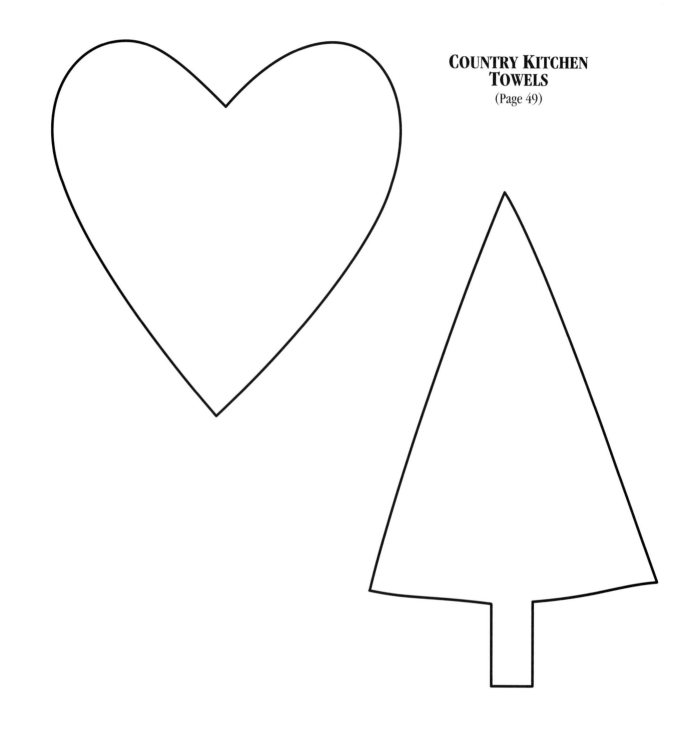

COUNTRY KITCHEN TOWELS
(Page 49)

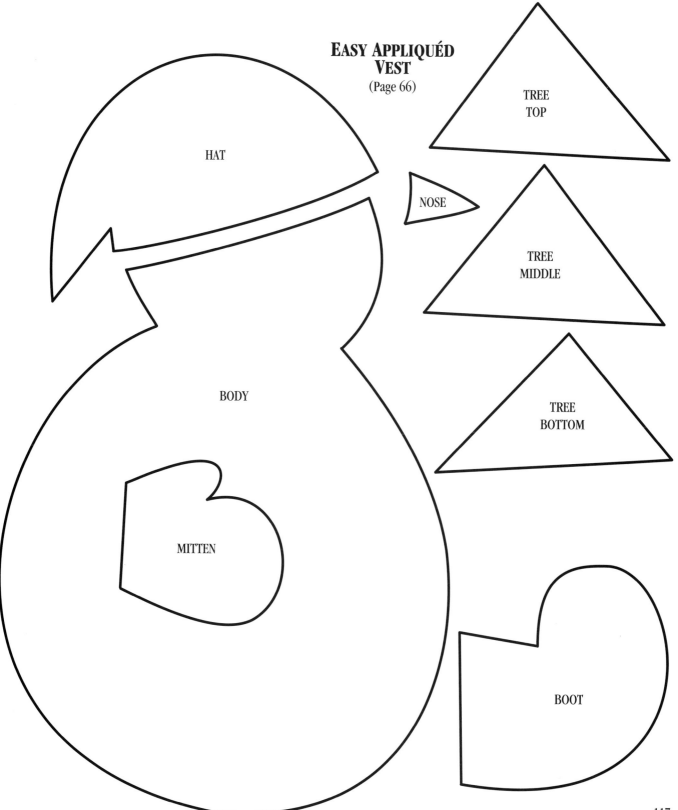

EASY APPLIQUÉD VEST
(Page 66)

HAT

NOSE

TREE TOP

TREE MIDDLE

TREE BOTTOM

BODY

MITTEN

BOOT

117

PATTERNS (continued)

CHOO-CHOO SWEATSHIRT AND COOKIES AND CANDY CARDIGAN
(Page 71)

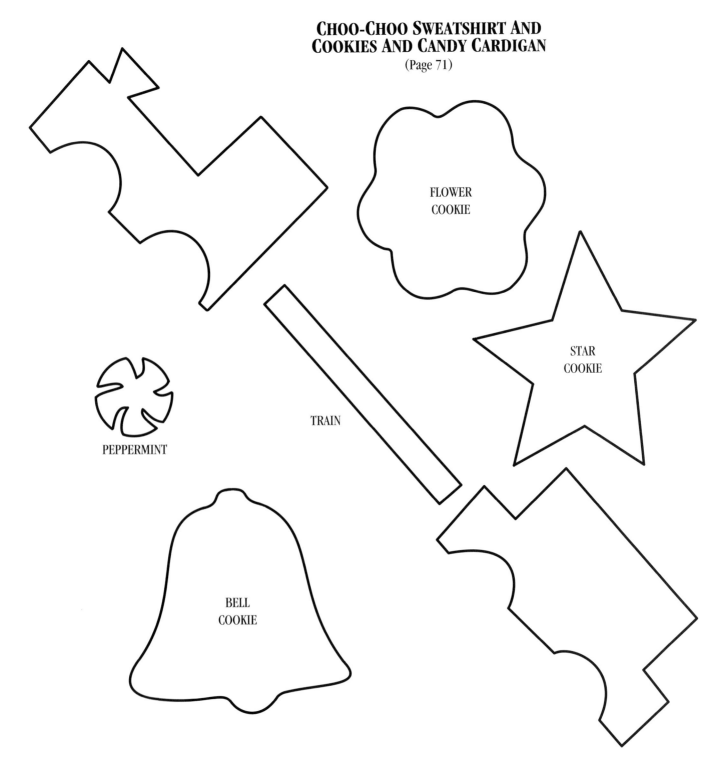

FLOWER
COOKIE

STAR
COOKIE

PEPPERMINT

TRAIN

BELL
COOKIE

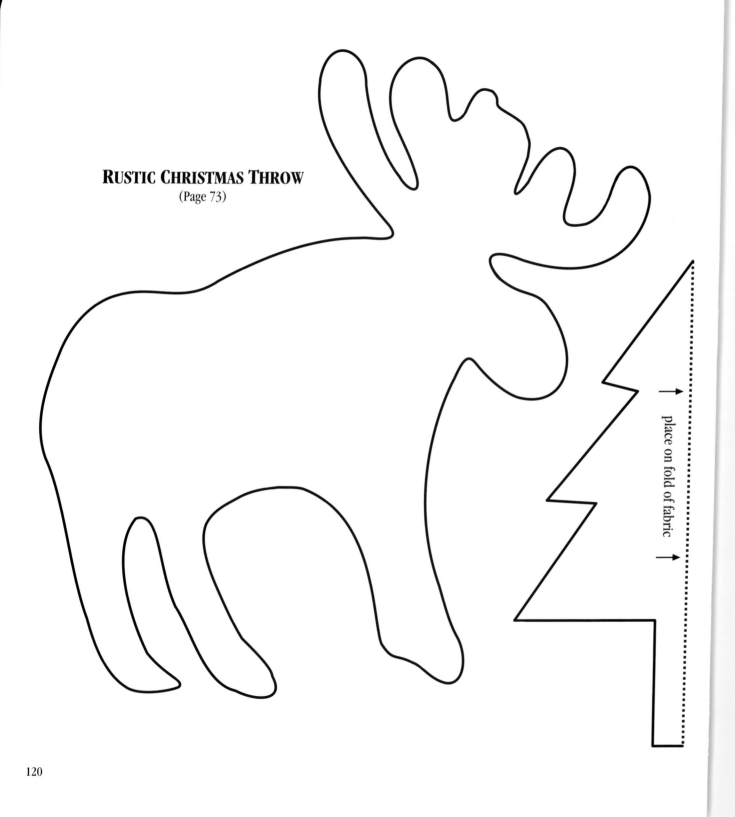

RUSTIC CHRISTMAS THROW
(Page 73)

place on fold of fabric

PATTERNS (continued)

RUSTIC CHRISTMAS THROW
(Page 73)

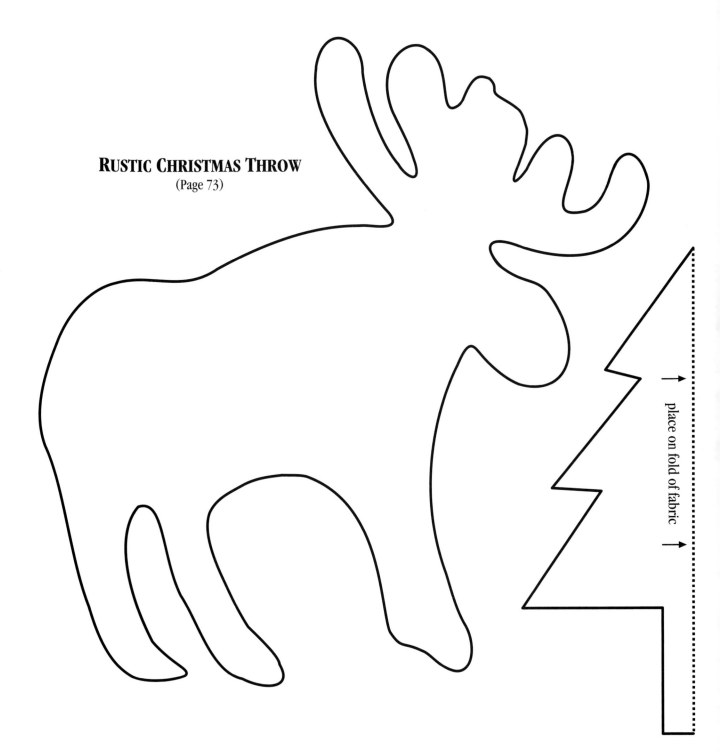

place on fold of fabric

CANDLELIGHT PLACE MATS

(Page 67)

KITCHEN TIPS

MEASURING INGREDIENTS

Liquid measuring cups have a rim above the measuring line to keep liquid ingredients from spilling. Nested measuring cups are used to measure dry ingredients, butter, shortening, and peanut butter. Measuring spoons are used for measuring both dry and liquid ingredients.

To measure flour or granulated sugar: Spoon ingredient into nested measuring cup and level off with a knife. Do not pack down with spoon.

To measure confectioners sugar: Sift sugar, spoon lightly into nested measuring cup, and level off with a knife.

To measure brown sugar: Pack sugar into nested measuring cup and level off with a knife. Sugar should hold its shape when removed from cup.

To measure dry ingredients equaling less than 1/4 cup: Dip measuring spoon into ingredient and level off with a knife.

To measure butter, shortening, or peanut butter: Pack ingredient firmly into nested measuring cup and level off with a knife.

To measure liquids: Use a liquid measuring cup placed on a flat surface. Pour ingredient into cup and check measuring line at eye level.

To measure honey or syrup: For a more accurate measurement, lightly spray measuring cup or spoon with cooking spray before measuring so the liquid will release easily from cup or spoon.

SOFTENING BUTTER OR MARGARINE

To soften butter, remove wrapper from butter and place on a microwave-safe plate. Microwave 1 stick 20 to 30 seconds at medium-low power (30%).

SOFTENING CREAM CHEESE

To soften cream cheese, remove wrapper from cream cheese and place on a microwave-safe plate. Microwave 1 to 1 1/2 minutes at medium power (50%) for one 8-ounce package or 30 to 45 seconds for one 3-ounce package.

SUBSTITUTING HERBS

To substitute fresh herbs for dried, use 1 tablespoon fresh chopped herbs for 1/2 teaspoon dried herbs.

SHREDDING CHEESE

To shred cheese easily, place wrapped cheese in freezer for 10 to 20 minutes before shredding.

TOASTING NUTS

To toast nuts, spread nuts on an ungreased baking sheet. Stirring occasionally, bake nuts in a preheated 350-degree oven 8 to 10 minutes or until slightly darker in color.

PREPARING CITRUS FRUIT ZEST

To remove outer portion of peel (colored part) from citrus fruits, use a fine grater or fruit zester, being careful not to cut into the bitter white portion. Zest is also referred to as grated peel in recipes.

USING CHOCOLATE

Chocolate is best stored in a cool, dry place. Since it has a high content of cocoa butter, chocolate may develop a grey film or "bloom" when temperatures change. This grey film does not affect the taste.

When melting chocolate, a low temperature is important to prevent overheating and scorching that will affect flavor and texture. The following are methods for melting chocolate:

Chocolate can be melted in a heavy saucepan over low heat, stirring constantly until melted.

Melting chocolate in a double boiler over hot, not boiling, water is a good method to prevent chocolate from overheating.

Using a microwave to melt chocolate is fast and convenient. To microwave chocolate, place in a microwave-safe container on medium-high power (80%) 1 minute; stir with a dry spoon. Continue to microwave 15 seconds at a time, stirring chocolate after each interval until smooth. Frequent stirring is important, as the chocolate will appear not to be melting, but will be soft when stirred. A shiny appearance is another sign that chocolate is melting.

GENERAL INSTRUCTIONS

TRACING PATTERNS

When one-half of pattern (indicated by dashed line on pattern) is shown, fold tracing paper in half and place fold along dashed line of pattern. Trace pattern half, including all placement symbols and markings; turn folded paper over and draw over all markings. Unfold pattern and lay flat. Cut out pattern along drawn lines.

When entire pattern is shown, place tracing paper over pattern and trace pattern, including all placement symbols and markings. Cut out pattern along drawn lines.

STENCILING

1. For stencil, cut a piece of acetate 1" larger on all sides than entire pattern. Center acetate over pattern and use permanent felt-tip pen with fine point to trace pattern. Place acetate piece on cutting mat and use craft knife to cut out stencil, making sure edges are smooth.

2. (**Note:** If desired, use removable tape to mask any cutout areas on stencil next to area being painted.) Hold or tape stencil in place. Use a clean, dry stencil brush for each color of paint. Dip brush in paint and remove excess on a paper towel. Brush should be almost dry to produce good results. Beginning at edge of cutout area, apply paint in a stamping motion. If desired, shade design by stamping additional paint around edge of cutout area. Carefully remove stencil and allow paint to dry.

CROSS STITCH
COUNTED CROSS STITCH (X)

Work 1 Cross Stitch to correspond to each colored square in the chart. For horizontal rows, work stitches in 2 journeys (**Fig. 1**). For vertical rows, complete each stitch as shown in **Fig. 2**. When the chart shows a

Backstitch crossing a colored square (**Fig. 3**), a Cross Stitch (**Fig. 1 or 2**) should be worked first; then the Backstitch (**Fig. 5**) should be worked on top of the Cross Stitch.

Fig. 1

Fig. 2

Fig. 3

QUARTER STITCH (¼X)

Quarter Stitches are denoted by triangular shapes of color in the chart and color key. Come up at 1 (**Fig. 4**); then split fabric thread to go down at 2.

Fig. 4

BACKSTITCH (B'ST)

For outline detail, Backstitch (shown in chart and color key by black or colored straight lines) should be worked after design has been completed (**Fig. 5**).

Fig. 5

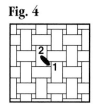

EMBROIDERY
RUNNING STITCH

Make a series of straight stitches with stitch length equal to the space between stitches (**Fig. 1**).

Fig. 1

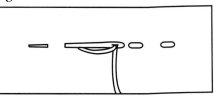

BLANKET STITCH

Referring to **Fig. 2**, come up at 1. Go down at 2 and come up at 3, keeping thread below point of needle. Continue working in this manner, going down at even numbers and coming up at odd numbers (**Fig. 3**).

Fig. 2   **Fig. 3**

FRENCH KNOT

Bring needle up at 1. Wrap thread once around needle and insert needle at 2, holding end of thread with non-stitching fingers (**Fig. 4**). Tighten knot; then pull needle through fabric, holding thread until it must be released. For a larger knot, use more strands; wrap only once.

Fig. 4

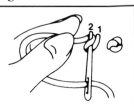

KITCHEN TIPS

MEASURING INGREDIENTS

Liquid measuring cups have a rim above the measuring line to keep liquid ingredients from spilling. Nested measuring cups are used to measure dry ingredients, butter, shortening, and peanut butter. Measuring spoons are used for measuring both dry and liquid ingredients.

To measure flour or granulated sugar: Spoon ingredient into nested measuring cup and level off with a knife. Do not pack down with spoon.

To measure confectioners sugar: Sift sugar, spoon lightly into nested measuring cup, and level off with a knife.

To measure brown sugar: Pack sugar into nested measuring cup and level off with a knife. Sugar should hold its shape when removed from cup.

To measure dry ingredients equaling less than 1/4 cup: Dip measuring spoon into ingredient and level off with a knife.

To measure butter, shortening, or peanut butter: Pack ingredient firmly into nested measuring cup and level off with a knife.

To measure liquids: Use a liquid measuring cup placed on a flat surface. Pour ingredient into cup and check measuring line at eye level.

To measure honey or syrup: For a more accurate measurement, lightly spray measuring cup or spoon with cooking spray before measuring so the liquid will release easily from cup or spoon.

SOFTENING BUTTER OR MARGARINE

To soften butter, remove wrapper from butter and place on a microwave-safe plate. Microwave 1 stick 20 to 30 seconds at medium-low power (30%).

SOFTENING CREAM CHEESE

To soften cream cheese, remove wrapper from cream cheese and place on a microwave-safe plate. Microwave 1 to 1 1/2 minutes at medium power (50%) for one 8-ounce package or 30 to 45 seconds for one 3-ounce package.

SUBSTITUTING HERBS

To substitute fresh herbs for dried, use 1 tablespoon fresh chopped herbs for 1/2 teaspoon dried herbs.

SHREDDING CHEESE

To shred cheese easily, place wrapped cheese in freezer for 10 to 20 minutes before shredding.

TOASTING NUTS

To toast nuts, spread nuts on an ungreased baking sheet. Stirring occasionally, bake nuts in a preheated 350-degree oven 8 to 10 minutes or until slightly darker in color.

PREPARING CITRUS FRUIT ZEST

To remove outer portion of peel (colored part) from citrus fruits, use a fine grater or fruit zester, being careful not to cut into the bitter white portion. Zest is also referred to as grated peel in recipes.

USING CHOCOLATE

Chocolate is best stored in a cool, dry place. Since it has a high content of cocoa butter, chocolate may develop a grey film or "bloom" when temperatures change. This grey film does not affect the taste.

When melting chocolate, a low temperature is important to prevent overheating and scorching that will affect flavor and texture. The following are methods for melting chocolate:

Chocolate can be melted in a heavy saucepan over low heat, stirring constantly until melted.

Melting chocolate in a double boiler over hot, not boiling, water is a good method to prevent chocolate from overheating.

Using a microwave to melt chocolate is fast and convenient. To microwave chocolate, place in a microwave-safe container on medium-high power (80%) 1 minute; stir with a dry spoon. Continue to microwave 15 seconds at a time, stirring chocolate after each interval until smooth. Frequent stirring is important, as the chocolate will appear not to be melting, but will be soft when stirred. A shiny appearance is another sign that chocolate is melting.

GENERAL INSTRUCTIONS

TRACING PATTERNS

When one-half of pattern (indicated by dashed line on pattern) is shown, fold tracing paper in half and place fold along dashed line of pattern. Trace pattern half, including all placement symbols and markings; turn folded paper over and draw over all markings. Unfold pattern and lay flat. Cut out pattern along drawn lines.

When entire pattern is shown, place tracing paper over pattern and trace pattern, including all placement symbols and markings. Cut out pattern along drawn lines.

STENCILING

1. For stencil, cut a piece of acetate 1" larger on all sides than entire pattern. Center acetate over pattern and use permanent felt-tip pen with fine point to trace pattern. Place acetate piece on cutting mat and use craft knife to cut out stencil, making sure edges are smooth.
2. (**Note:** If desired, use removable tape to mask any cutout areas on stencil next to area being painted.) Hold or tape stencil in place. Use a clean, dry stencil brush for each color of paint. Dip brush in paint and remove excess on a paper towel. Brush should be almost dry to produce good results. Beginning at edge of cutout area, apply paint in a stamping motion. If desired, shade design by stamping additional paint around edge of cutout area. Carefully remove stencil and allow paint to dry.

CROSS STITCH
COUNTED CROSS STITCH (X)

Work 1 Cross Stitch to correspond to each colored square in the chart. For horizontal rows, work stitches in 2 journeys (**Fig. 1**). For vertical rows, complete each stitch as shown in **Fig. 2**. When the chart shows a

Backstitch crossing a colored square (**Fig. 3**), a Cross Stitch (**Fig. 1 or 2**) should be worked first; then the Backstitch (**Fig. 5**) should be worked on top of the Cross Stitch.

Fig. 1

Fig. 2

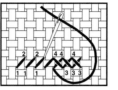

Fig. 3

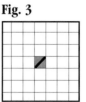

QUARTER STITCH (¼X)

Quarter Stitches are denoted by triangular shapes of color in the chart and color key. Come up at 1 (**Fig. 4**); then split fabric thread to go down at 2.

Fig. 4

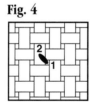

BACKSTITCH (B'ST)

For outline detail, Backstitch (shown in chart and color key by black or colored straight lines) should be worked after design has been completed (**Fig. 5**).

Fig. 5

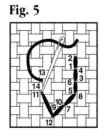

EMBROIDERY
RUNNING STITCH

Make a series of straight stitches with stitch length equal to the space between stitches (**Fig. 1**).

Fig. 1

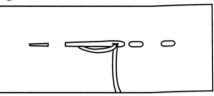

BLANKET STITCH

Referring to **Fig. 2**, come up at 1. Go down at 2 and come up at 3, keeping thread below point of needle. Continue working in this manner, going down at even numbers and coming up at odd numbers (**Fig. 3**).

Fig. 2   Fig. 3

FRENCH KNOT

Bring needle up at 1. Wrap thread once around needle and insert needle at 2, holding end of thread with non-stitching fingers (**Fig. 4**). Tighten knot; then pull needle through fabric, holding thread until it must be released. For a larger knot, use more strands; wrap only once.

Fig. 4

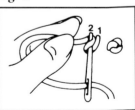

EQUIVALENT MEASUREMENTS

1 tablespoon	=	3 teaspoons
1/8 cup (1 fluid ounce)	=	2 tablespoons
1/4 cup (2 fluid ounces)	=	4 tablespoons
1/3 cup	=	5 1/3 tablespoons
1/2 cup (4 fluid ounces)	=	8 tablespoons
3/4 cup (6 fluid ounces)	=	12 tablespoons
1 cup (8 fluid ounces)	=	16 tablespoons or 1/2 pint
2 cups (16 fluid ounces)	=	1 pint
1 quart (32 fluid ounces)	=	2 pints
1/2 gallon (64 fluid ounces)	=	2 quarts
1 gallon (128 fluid ounces)	=	4 quarts

HELPFUL FOOD EQUIVALENTS

1/2 cup butter	=	1 stick butter
1 square baking chocolate	=	1 ounce chocolate
1 cup chocolate chips	=	6 ounces chocolate chips
2 1/4 cups packed brown sugar	=	1 pound brown sugar
3 1/2 cups unsifted confectioners sugar	=	1 pound confectioners sugar
2 cups granulated sugar	=	1 pound granulated sugar
4 cups all-purpose flour	=	1 pound all-purpose flour
1 cup shredded cheese	=	4 ounces cheese
3 cups sliced carrots	=	1 pound carrots
1/2 cup chopped celery	=	1 rib celery
1/2 cup chopped onion	=	1 medium onion
1 cup chopped green pepper	=	1 large green pepper

RECIPE INDEX

A

APPETIZERS AND SNACKS:
Cheesy Crab Toasts, 103
Curried Snack Sticks, 92
Nutty Butterscotch Popcorn, 82
Stuffed Gouda Cheese, 102
Zesty Ripe Olive Dip, 103
Apricot-Nut Fruitcake, 113

B

Bacon-Mushroom Casserole, 81
Berry Christmas Jam, 89
BEVERAGES:
Champagne Punch, 107
Cranberry Freezer Daiquiris, 102
Glühwein, 95
Raspberry Cider, 113
Raspberry Cream Liqueur, 79
Spiced Coffee Mix, 105
BREADS:
Brownie Nut Bread, 106
Herbed Christmas Rolls, 110
Southwest Olive Bread, 102
Brownie Nut Bread, 106

C

CANDIES:
Chocolate Granola Candies, 87
Chocolate-Dipped Peppermint Sticks, 91
Christmas Candy Lollipops, 97
Dried Fruit-Nut Rolls, 85
Nutty Maple Fudge, 76
Rocky Road Candy, 99
Champagne Punch, 107
Cheese Danish Pastries, 104

Cheesy Crab Toasts, 103
Chocolate Cinnamon Rolls, 104
Chocolate Granola Candies, 87
Chocolate-Covered Cherry Pie, 77
Chocolate-Dipped Peppermint Sticks, 91
Christmas Candy Lollipops, 97
CONDIMENTS:
Berry Christmas Jam, 89
Cranberry-Orange Jelly, 97
Creamy Cinnamon Spread, 106
Jezebel Sauce, 83
COOKIES
Fruitcake Cookies, 99
Gingerbread Bars, 93
Cranberry Freezer Daiquiris, 102
Cranberry-Orange Gelatin Salad, 111
Cranberry-Orange Jelly, 97
Creamy Cinnamon Spread, 106
Curried Snack Sticks, 92

D-E

DESSERTS (See also Candies, Cookies, and Pies):
Apricot-Nut Fruitcake, 113
Holiday Ice Cream, 107
Dried Fruit-Nut Rolls, 85
ENTRÉES:
Bacon-Mushroom Casserole, 81
Sweet-and-Sour Pork Chops, 102
Turkey and Dressing Ring, 110

F-G

Fruitcake Cookies, 99
Fruited Sweet Potato Casserole, 111
Fudge-Topped Pumpkin Pie, 113
Gingerbread Bars, 93
Glühwein, 95
Green Beans au Gratin, 110

H-N

Herbed Christmas Rolls, 110
Holiday Ice Cream, 107
Jezebel Sauce, 83
Nutty Butterscotch Popcorn, 82
Nutty Fudge Pie, 105
Nutty Maple Fudge, 76

P-R

PASTRIES:
Cheese Danish Pastries, 104
Chocolate Cinnamon Rolls, 104
PIES:
Chocolate-Covered Cherry Pie, 77
Fudge-Topped Pumpkin Pie, 113
Nutty Fudge Pie, 105
Raspberry Cider, 113
Raspberry Cream Liqueur, 79
Rocky Road Candy, 99

S-Z

Southwest Olive Bread, 102
Spiced Coffee Mix, 105
Stuffed Gouda Cheese, 102
Sweet-and-Sour Pork Chops, 102
Turkey and Dressing Ring, 110
VEGETABLES AND SIDE DISHES:
Cranberry-Orange Gelatin Salad, 111
Fruited Sweet Potato Casserole, 111
Green Beans Au Gratin, 110
Zesty Ripe Olive Dip, 103

CREDITS

We want to extend a warm *thank you* to the generous people who allowed us to photograph our projects in their homes:

- *Cheery Country Kitchen:* Nancy Gunn Porter
- *A Golden Celebration:* Martha Bradshaw
- *Easy Elegance:* Martha Bradshaw
- *Homespun Charm:* Nancy Gunn Porter
- *Visions of Sugarplums:* Nancy Gunn Porter
- *Welcoming Wreaths:* Nancy Gunn Porter
- *Rustic Santa:* Nancy Gunn Porter
- *A Touch of Victoriana:* Richard and Susan Wildung

We also want to thank Nancy Gunn Porter and Shirley Held for allowing us to photograph portions of *Gifts in a Jiffy* and *Treats in a Wink* in their homes.

To Magna IV Color Imaging of Little Rock, Arkansas, we say thank you for the superb color reproduction and excellent pre-press preparation.

We especially want to thank photographers Mark Mathews, Larry Pennington, Karen Shirey, and Ken West of Peerless Photography, and Jerry R. Davis of Jerry Davis Photography, all of Little Rock, Arkansas, for their time, patience, and excellent work.

To the talented people who helped in the creation of the following projects in this book, we extend a special word of thanks:

- *Crocheted Fabric Tree Skirt,* page 28: Dorothy Frantz
- *Christmas Candles Sweatshirt,* page 56: Kay Bagley and Cindy Moore
- *Festive Socks,* page 59: Maryanne Moreck
- *Double-Strand Diamond Afghan,* page 63: Carole Rutter Tippett
- *Christmas Mini Totes,* page 91: Ann Townsend
- *Bargello Mug,* page 95: Teal Lee Elliott

We extend a sincere *thank you* to the people who assisted in making and testing the projects in this book: Jo Ann Bowling, Judy Crowder, Pat Johnson, Risa Johnson, Kathy Jones, Sheila Karnes, Christel Shelton, Cathy Smith, and Karen Tyler.